Encounters
Exploring Christia...

Encounters:
Exploring Christian Faith

edited by

MICHAEL MAYNE
Vicar of Great St Mary's, Cambridge

Darton, Longman and Todd
London

First published in 1986 by
Darton, Longman and Todd Ltd
89 Lillie Road, London SW6 1UD

© 1986 Church of Great St Mary's, Cambridge

ISBN 0 232 51669 3

British Library Cataloguing in Publication Data

Encounters: exploring Christian faith.
  1. Christian life 2. Faith
  I. Mayne, Michael
  248.4   BV4509.5

ISBN 0–232–51669–3

Phototypeset by Input Typesetting Ltd, London SW19 8DR
Printed and bound in Great Britain by
Anchor Brendon Ltd, Tiptree, Essex

Contents

Contributors

ROBERT RUNCIE, enthroned as the 102nd Archbishop of Canterbury in 1980, was previously Dean of Trinity Hall, Cambridge, Principal of Cuddesdon Theological College, and Bishop of St Albans.

EAMON DUFFY is a lay Roman Catholic, a Church historian within the Cambridge Faculty of Theology, and a Fellow of Magdalene College.

JACK DOMINIAN, one of Britain's leading Roman Catholic laymen, is Consultant Psychiatrist at the Central Middlesex Hospital, Director of the Marital Research Centre, and a writer on sex and marriage.

COLIN MORRIS, author and broadcaster, is a former missionary in Zambia and Minister of Wesley's Chapel. He has served as President of the Methodist Conference, and is currently Head of Religious Broadcasting at the BBC.

DAVID SHEPPARD has spend his whole ministry in the inner city, as Warden of the Mayflower Centre in Camden Town, as Bishop of Woolwich, and since 1975 as Bishop of Liverpool.

DEREK WORLOCK was consecrated Roman Catholic Bishop of Portsmouth in 1965. He was transplanted to Liverpool in 1976 as its Archbishop where, with Bishop David Sheppard, he has made a vigorous stand on social issues.

PETER BALL was one of the founders of the Community of the Glorious Ascension and served as its Prior for seventeen years. He was made Bishop of Lewes in 1977.

UNA KROLL is a deaconess, writer and broadcaster. She has worked as a doctor in London and Africa. She is now working in Sussex.

TIMOTHY RADCLIFFE is Prior of Blackfriars in Oxford where he teaches Scripture. He is a former Chaplain to the University of London.

MYRA BLYTH trained at Regents Park Baptist College in Oxford before working as Assistant Minister at Sutton Baptist Church. She is now Youth Secretary for the British Council of Churches.

Foreword

There are those who say that university missions belong to the past and to a less secularised generation. Today's undergraduates are neither interested enough in the Christian faith nor responsive enough to traditional modes of presentation.

But the success of *Encounters*, the interest and response it engendered, tells a different story. The quality of the addresses, the concentration of those who came to listen, the liveliness of the discussions which followed – all these signify concern for the questions of the spirit, and a confidence that the Christian faith is worth exploring.

At the start of a similar week a generation ago, Archbishop William Temple gave this advice to his fellow missioners: 'Let us take care that nothing we say or do makes Christ appear unattractive'. That's the best advice of all: whether the writers in *Encounters* have taken it to heart is for the reader to judge. There are certainly signs to suggest that many in Cambridge must have thought so.

ROBERT CANTUAR

Introduction

For eight days in February 1985 the University Church and
the Roman Catholic chaplaincy in Cambridge were the centre
for an ecumenical exploration of the Christian faith. Some
called it a mission; others a teaching week; those who planned
it – initially a committee representing the college deans and
chaplains – chose to call it *Encounters*.

What did we have in mind?

A presentation of Christian belief which was at once
personal and infectious; thought-provoking and honest; an
interpretation of life which took account of its *mystery* and its
frequently daunting mixture of good and evil. We therefore
chose speakers from a variety of traditions whose theological
understanding was combined with a pastoral experience
which had taught them to communicate at a human level,
and who would demonstrate that only a form of belief which
fully engages the mind as well as the heart can survive in the
real world, where the innocent suffer and where those we love
fall ill and die. And who did not claim to know all the answers.

In his opening address the Archbishop of Canterbury
struck just this note when he claimed that the great strength of
Christianity is that 'it does not attempt to explain everything.
There is always at its core . . . a heart of mystery'. Dr Eamon
Duffy, in speaking of what it feels like 'when belief fails',
also asserted that there is often no answer to life's many
perplexities, yet warned that if we 'exclude wonder and reverence as legitimate human responses to the world . . . [then]
men and women . . . will cease to speak of God'.

Each spoke of the ultimate mystery, of God disclosed in
Jesus Christ, God identified 'with the weakness and nakedness

1

of the suffering figure on the cross'; of how, in the end, 'in spite of appearances the world is very good'.

We hoped that *Encounters* would attract not only Christian students wanting to grow in their understanding of the Christian mysteries, but those who were agnostic or just plain inquisitive. Not least, we wanted people to understand better the legitimate breadth and space of faith and discipleship and the need for diverse and complementary insights in our encounter with God. So often the Church seems to deter people from exploring the truth by giving the impression that we must affirm some credal belief at the outset. Yet many of us in fact start our inward journey very tentatively, in response to a deeply felt but ill-defined need for God, and it is in our encounters with other Christians, in listening to sermons or taking part in acts of worship, that we come slowly to discover that we cannot avoid the mysterious claim that God is made known in the man Jesus Christ, and that life is illuminated by his passion and his cross.

We asked the speakers to be as personal as they wished in describing their own encounter with God and how that affects the encounter with other people: in Colin Morris's words, the way we look upon others through the eyes of Jesus; and the way we look for Jesus in others.

What did *Encounters* achieve for some of the hundreds who came and heard these addresses? Only God knows. An encounter may be a chance, often unexpected, meeting. It may lead nowhere, alter nothing; but it may change your life. God's encounter with us may come in those unexpected disclosures – certain words or actions, a sudden glimpse of authentic goodness – which take us out of ourselves and reveal a reality and a truth we had not previously seen.

MICHAEL MAYNE
Great St Mary's
Cambridge

1

Encountering God: why I believe

In the first two chapters the Archbishop of Canterbury, Dr ROBERT RUNCIE, sets out the reasons for his own faith. In the first he defines, defends and justifies his belief in God; in the second he goes on to explore the content of that belief and the nature of faith, which begins with the giving of attention to God's action in Christ and an act of trust.

Father Harry Williams, formerly Dean of Trinity College, Cambridge, records in his biography a memory of William Temple preaching one Sunday evening, in the course of a University Mission: 'I could hardly understand a word, but the sight of an Archbishop in his robes uttering a ceaseless stream of words in a rotund style and fruity voice absolutely mesmerised me. From that moment I knew I wanted to be a clergyman'.[1]

Let me say straight away that this kind of conversion experience is not the sort of thing I shall be aiming to produce. I remember Billy Graham in Cambridge in 1954. I fell for his preaching because he told such marvellous stories. To illustrate the need to be highly motivated, he told of the man who, strolling across a graveyard in the dark, fell into a deep grave which had been prepared for the next day's funeral. Try as he would the sides were so steep he could not get out, and he sank back exhausted. Some time later another man crossed the same graveyard and he too fell in. Thinking himself alone and frightened he struggled to grapple up the sides. The first man leant forward and touched him and said, 'Son, you won't get out of here!' 'But oh boy, he did!' But

3

within such preaching I have to say he preached Jesus Christ with all the vibrant attraction of his call to us to decide for him.

We are concerned here to explore some fundamental questions about Truth, the existence of God, human destiny, the nature of man – indeed the meaning of life itself. These are fundamental questions, and not to be ignored or dodged. They continue to be asked, despite having been frequently declared meaningless or impossible to answer.

Faith is often the only form of response appropriate to these kinds of ultimate questions. By faith I do not mean an irrational reaction of blind optimism or homespun philosophy displayed by the immature when confronted by complex or trying circumstances. 'It will all turn out for the best, it will all make sense, in the end.' Faith is perhaps more the ability to say 'Yes' to such questions as 'Is there intelligibility, order and purpose in the universe?'

As an undergraduate I well remember Isaiah Berlin telling us it was our duty not to spend our lives lying on a bed of unexamined assumptions. I think one assumption people might be tempted to make is that an archbishop has 'made it' spiritually: he knows what it is all about, he has all the answers.

I would like to examine that assumption. Because I am an archbishop it is obvious that I believe, that I live by faith. But I believe that everybody lives by faith of some kind – only some have articulated and explored their commitment more thoroughly than others. I am here to try to tell you why I believe in God, and find my faith through the Christian way.

Perhaps I should digress just a little and say why, today, I think it is so important that I believe. I was once startled by Bishop Desmond Tutu saying to me, 'I always find it very hard to be a Christian in England, the issues are so blurred: in South Africa everything is so clear-cut.' It does seem to me that audible clashes of principle or the oppressions of tyranny can lead to a clearer perception of spiritual values and the meaning of life – look at Poland and how

4

it has responded to the death of the outspoken priest Fr Popieluszko.

But in Britain we are more inclined to spiritual stagnation: both great sanctity and spectacular wickedness are in short supply. Perhaps we should thank God for the latter. But what of the former? Somehow the Church must be spiritually awakened to hear God's voice speaking through today's events and discoveries – otherwise it will end by speaking only to itself. Some time ago I found myself wondering whether the language used in reporting Terry Waite's operation in Libya (words like 'mission', 'faith', and 'miracle') was merely the residue to a decaying Christianity, or the reflection of an unspoken need for spiritual values to be reasserted.

I believe there *is* an underlying yearning for God and for things spiritual. I shall speak more of this later. I am not (altogether) convinced that it is (or need be) a case of enter progress, exit God; nor that the present-day substitutes for religion (Communism, nationalism, materialism, humanism) will ultimately replace true religion and religious belief. However, we may have to work harder than we do at present to ensure that a sense of religious mystery surrounds our secular humanitarian activities, and that a sense of religious obligation tempers and disciplines our selfishness, if we are to avoid national suicide.

For me it is Christianity which makes sense of more things about the world and about myself than any ideology. But Christianity is not a once for all religion, handed to me on a plate at baptism, completely ready-made, final. One of its greatest strengths is that it does not attempt to explain everything. There is always at its core, as in every relationship, a heart of mystery.

The God who enters into a personal relation with us through Christ is a God of ultimate mystery. We know that saints like John of the Cross and, nearer home, Mother Julian of Norwich, wrestled with these mysteries; there are records of their agonies of mind and heart as their thinking about God was purified in prayer and tested in suffering. But they found a faith deeper than would have been possible had they remained superficial and conventional.

5

Most of us are at times like the poet Francis Thompson in 'The Hound of Heaven' – we flee from God when things are hard and the light of faith is flickering. And yet at such times we can say, with the man in the gospels, 'Lord, I believe – help thou my unbelief', trying to make our muted, half-hearted 'Yes' into a fully articulated response that can shape and rule our lives.

These are some of the reasons why I think it is important to believe. But I do not think I have yet approached the question *why* I believe closely enough. Nor indeed am I sure this is exactly what I am going to do. I think there is a risk in telling or explaining why I believe in God. And the risk is that the God in whom I believe may be obscured or distorted when I state my reasons for believing in him, just as trying to explain why I love a person by describing a particular attribute or talent may imply that they are loved for the attribute or talent rather than for themselves. (So you can tell your girl friend as often as you like *that* you love her, but it's sometimes dangerous to tell her *why* you love her!)

If I say, for instance, that I believe in God because my prayers have sometimes been answered, then I may well be taken to mean that I believe in the existence of an invisible slot-machine which can sometimes provide me with what I want. And if I say that I believe in God because a friend recovered from cancer when all the doctors had given up hope, I may well seem to be saying that I believe in the existence and effectiveness of an occult healing-power.

So the God in whom I believe may be, or seem to be, nothing more than my reason for believing in him. I think there are some people of whom this is true: their God simply *is* their reason for believing in him. There is – or was very recently – a well-known American evangelist who regularly appeared on the TV dripping with jewellery, even to the extent of having diamonds set in his teeth! His message was, 'I believe in God, and see how richly he has blessed me. If you believe in him you too will be rich.' The God he preaches is nothing more than the source of riches to those who believe in him.

But I am sure that to most people the God in whom they believe is not simply an answering machine or an occult power-source – just as the person whom they love is not simply a nice voice combined with a talent for dancing and one or two other things. The difficulty is that the more precisely we set out our reasons for believing the more risk we take of suggesting that these reasons for our belief are the actual substance of our belief.

And here lies the danger of putting forward as our reasons for belief those classical arguments or proofs for the existence of God with which some of you will be familiar. They are claimed – and perhaps justifiably – to be logical demonstrations that, for instance, a First Cause must exist and a most Perfect Being must exist. But if they are our reasons for believing in God, then the God we believe in is (or at least seems to be) no more than a First Cause or a most Perfect Being. Well, I suppose one could believe in a God who was simply that, but it would be a very dim and dull and abstract kind of belief. It would not make much difference to anything, and it would hardly be worth recommending to anybody else. It would be no great achievement to persuade an atheist or agnostic to admit the existence of a First Cause or a Perfect Being.

Yes, in making explicit the reasons why we believe in God there is a risk of misleading people about the kind of God we believe in. Just as the safest (and probably most truthful) answer to someone who asks *why* you love him or her is, 'Just because I do, and I can't help it', so the safest, and perhaps the most honest, course for me would be to say, 'Why do I believe in God? . . . Just because I do – and I can't help it', and, having said that, to go on at once to what I believe. But there is rather more to be said.

Let us go back to this business of loving. I do not apologise for doing so – for believing in God is much more like loving someone than it is like believing there is oil in a certain rock stratum or life on a certain planet. You cannot really say why you love someone, and that all this business about her seductive voice, her shapely figure, fails to express or contain the heart of the matter. But let us suppose someone said: 'You *can't* love Susan. She's no sense of humour at all'; or, 'You shouldn't love Susan. She tells lies.' Well, you might respond with a fist or a kick on the shins, or you might say, 'I know that, but I still love her.' But more likely, especially if the speaker was someone you respected, you would say: 'Susan does have a sense of humour, but it's very subtle and it's not everyone who notices it'; or, 'Susan doesn't tell lies: it's just that she forgets and gets things muddled up.' These words do not give the reason why you love Susan, but they do give the reason why it is not foolish or improper to love her. They do not explain your love – but they do to some degree defend it and justify it.

Similarly I cannot satisfactorily explain why I believe in God, but I can, at least to some extent, defend and justify my belief. I can say, first and with great conviction, that there is *space* for belief in God: huge space, empty space, sensible space, that is almost crying out to be filled.

It is the space of which we are aware when we *wonder at the mystery* of being. By this I do not just mean wonder at the beauty and order of the world, but something more fundamental than that – wonder at the fact that there is anything at all. Wittgenstein wrote in the *Tractatus*, 'The mystical is not *how* the world is but *that* it is', and in a paper on ethics he referred to occasions when he found himself wondering at the existence of the world and saying to himself, 'How remarkable that the world exists, how remarkable that *anything* exists.'[2] Yes, we may trace with increasing scientific precision the 'how' of the world, detect evermore exactly the laws and forces which determine its operations and its history, but *that* the world exists, *that* those laws and forces are there, remains a matter for undiminished wonder.

And a still greater matter for wonder is my own presence and awareness and consciousness within the world at which I wonder. Here am I, within the mystery, sensing and seeing the mystery, treading on and handling and making use of the mystery – surviving, one might say, by courtesy of the mystery. It cannot be the height of wisdom simply to swim and swan around within the mystery in mindless oblivion. Nor, on the other hand, can it be foolish to have some kind of attitude to the mystery. And to take a certain attitude at this profound level is, I think, certainly the beginning, and possibly even the core and centre, of belief in God. To perceive and respond to the mystery as a *gracious* mystery would be to have an implicit belief in God. So, there is certainly space – intellectual space – for belief in God.

Now comes the second point of my defence. It lies in the special and remarkable character of moral awareness. Kant said there are two things which move mankind to wonder – the starry heavens above and the moral law within. I suppose that by 'wonder at the starry heavens' Kant meant what I have just been thinking of – wonder at the mystery of being. It is when we look up at the night sky and think of its immensity and of our minuteness that the mystery of being is most profoundly experienced.

By 'wonder at the moral law within' I think Kant meant what I would describe, rather less imposingly, as 'wonder at the fact that things matter'. 'A man's morality', says Iris Murdoch, 'is not only his choices but his vision.'[3] And the cause for wonder, for vision, is not that things matter to me – subjectively. It is that some things matter objectively, they have a right to matter, and that this is so absolute and irrefutable.

The famine in Ethiopia may or may not matter to me: but there is no doubt that it has a right to matter and that, though I and billions of others may be indifferent, it would still have a right to matter. This right confronts us, and if we ignore it it judges and condemns us. In our awareness the world is not simply registered, as it might be on a spool of film or a tape-recorder. At times it confronts us as mattering; it demands from us some kind of response and condemns us if that response is not forthcoming. There are times when the moral imperative is clear and practical: feeding the hungry, freeing the prisoner, protesting against nuclear weapons or racial discrimination, starting a movement like Amnesty International or Christian Aid.

Moral philosophers may argue as to why – in terms of what

general ethical principles – the famine in Ethiopia matters and makes its demands on us, but they can hardly deny that it does so. And so do many other things – public and private, large or small. Our awareness that certain things have a right to matter is as indisputable as our awareness that they exist.

Try telling yourself that it does not matter that you have betrayed a friend, stolen a poor man's coat or, long ago, tortured for your pleasure a helpless cat. Would you buy a second-hand car from a moral philosopher who maintained that these things did not matter? Of course in different ages and societies the moral awareness is sensitive to different things, and in some people it has become atrophied and even, in pathological cases, non-existent. But the conviction that certain things have a right to matter is as widespread among mankind as the conviction that certain things exist.

In the authority with which certain things engage our moral awareness and make their demands there is again *space* – moral space – for belief in God: for the belief that moral demand springs from a source as profoundly mysterious and awesome as does the universe itself.

Let me repeat that I am not stating the reasons why I believe in God: I am simply setting out reasons why it is not foolish to believe – or naive or a mark of senility or wishful thinking. It is with this reminder that I come to the third of these reasons – which is Jesus Christ or, perhaps more exactly, the story of Jesus Christ. This, to put it over-simply, is claimed to be the story of God making himself present, making himself known in and to the world: and in it God is disclosed not as one who exercises a distant and detached supremacy over the world of his creation but as one who, in the greatness of his love for that world, pours out and expends himself 'unto death'.

That story really belongs to Chapter 2, but I mention it here for this reason. You may disbelieve the claim made for this story: you may disbelieve the story itself. But I doubt if anyone who seriously attends to the story and the claim made for it can dismiss the whole matter as foolish or trivial or irrelevant – as something of which the truth or falsehood would be immaterial, making no difference to our feeling and attitude about the world in general or our own place in it.

So in and through the story of Jesus Christ and the claims made about it there is again *space* for belief in God. This time I would call it emotional space: if we believe in the God disclosed in the story then there is met the most universal of all human needs – the need to be unconditionally accepted and totally loved.

Here is an illustration. Some time ago I took part in a discussion on transplant operations. A doctor described how that morning after a road accident in Vienna a kidney had been taken from a child's body, frozen, put on a plane and brought to London where he had put it into another person. 'But', he said, 'I couldn't do this work if I thought that I was simply dealing with a bundle of parts. I don't know how to define life and I'm not very religious, but what I have of faith reminds me that I must respect, no, reverence, every person with whom I have to do.'

It is easy to think of a person as a bundle of parts or a mixture of chemicals – but perhaps that is a case of beginning at the wrong end. See him as the object of God's love, and he comes together as a person. It is easy to see mankind as economic units or racial groups, and it falls apart. See it as the family for whom Christ died and there is emotional fulfilment – a space filled.

So I suppose I cannot say simply *why* I believe in God, but I can point to *space* for such belief – intellectual, moral and emotional space. This at least helps to make sense of Christian belief – belief for which (let me say finally) I remain profoundly grateful. I am thankful for whatever it may be – the example of others, experience of life, the direct touch of God upon me – which has led me to believe and sustained my belief against counter-pressures which are put upon it and against difficulties which are inherent in that belief itself. I do not want to end with pious platitudes about the blessedness of belief, but I have no doubt that if that belief were taken from me I should find the world an intellectual question mark, a moral vacuum and an emotional desert. And those things I firmly do not believe.

Notes

1. Harry Williams, *Some Day I'll Find You*. 1982.

2. Ludwig Wittgenstein, *Tractatus* (1922); N. Malcolm, *Ludwig Wittgenstein*. 1962.

3. Iris Murdoch, 'The Sovereignty of Good', in *The Sovereignty of Good and other Concepts*. 1970.

2

Encountering God: what I believe

In Chapter 1 I tried to say something about *why* I believe – in this chapter my theme is *what* I believe.

I believe in God through Jesus Christ. That is the heart of the matter. I believe in God as he is disclosed in Jesus Christ – as he meets the world and is met by the world in Jesus Christ. I do not believe that Jesus simply told us what God is like – as I might tell you what someone is like whom I know better. I believe that Jesus *was* what God is like, and that he shows us God rather as an entertainer who plays various roles on television might show me what he is really like by coming in person into my home. Let me put it another way: 'The divine story-teller, the Author of the story of the universe, has done what no novelist could possibly do and entered the story he is telling as one of the characters in it' (Christopher Bryant).[1]

This identity of being between God and Jesus is stated in Christian teaching, but it is not explained. No symbol, analogy or model can carry us any distance, and to my mind all attempts to explain this identity have a tendency only to erode it. I take it as a mystery as far beyond explanation as is the mystery of my own being and of the being of the world. Our safest eloquence is silence.

I believe that Jesus is Emmanuel – God with us, God incarnate, God living a human life. Therefore the story of Jesus is of supreme importance – the story of how he conducted himself and how he fared in the world. We do not know the whole story. All that has ever been reported about Jesus can have occupied no more than a small proportion of his thirty-three years. So there is a mist around the edge of the story. And there is a certain mistiness within the story too. However certain we are about what Jesus said and did in the gospels, we can no longer detect the precise tone of his voice, the ring of his words in the ears of those who heard them, or the significance of his actions in the eyes of those who saw them.

I must say I do not find this mistiness disturbing; and therefore I do not find it disturbing when informed and careful criticism raises doubts about the authenticity of certain incidents in the gospels, or certain sayings attributed to Jesus. Those doubts simply contribute a little to the general mistiness, and I can accept that uncertainty as I can accept the uncertainty of my memory of my father who died years ago. I have forgotten now much of what my father said and did, and I have discovered that certain things cannot have happened as I remember them. But I am entirely confident that the figure whom I see in my mind is the figure of my father: I still know what kind of man he was, and his particular manner and style, and the shape and quality of his life. So it is with the figure of Jesus.

Let me give you another illustration. When I was Bishop of St Albans there had been before me a bishop called Michael Furse, who was a great character. He had been a bishop exactly forty years before me, and people remembered him vividly. When I went to confirm children, grandparents would often say, 'I was confirmed by Bishop Furse – now he was a *real* bishop!' Sometimes people would tell me what he had said to them: 'What's the use of a banana out of the bunch? It goes bad, doesn't it?' 'The one who endures to the end shall be saved' was one of his favourite texts. I developed a clear picture of Mike Furse, and indeed there came a time when I felt I could almost have written one of his sermons. Sometimes when I was told something about him I would say, 'That can't be true – it doesn't fit in with what I've heard.'

I never met him, but the time between us was much the same as the time between the crucifixion and the gospel writers. Memories are strong enough in our day and they were much stronger in our Lord's. So I am not as sceptical as some about the accuracy of the portrait of Jesus we find in the New Testament.

None the less it does seem particularly appropriate that the figure should emerge from the gospels with a certain mistiness around it, for within the gospels Jesus is presented as a distinctly enigmatic figure. He enters without pomp or preparation into the most commonplace scenes of life, yet makes each scene his own. He is casual and unselective, even scandalous in the company he keeps, yet minutely attentive and sensitive to it. His total dedication to God is also easy and intimate. He lives in obedience to the Jewish tradition but presumes to judge it. He is often misunderstood even by those most intimate with him. He wins for himself wonder and admiration, but does not exploit what he has won, and as his fame and following increase he speaks of his rejection, suffering and death.

His life poses the persistent, nagging question: 'Who *is* this?' 'Who do men say that I am?' and the manner of his death proposes the answer, 'An offender, a pretender and blasphemer, a misleader of the people'.

Then there followed the resurrection. During the last fifty years, since Professor C. H. Dodd detected so conclusively the content of the very earliest Christian preaching, it has been difficult to take seriously the account of the origins of Christianity which, up to then, had been widely taught by liberal theologians. They argued that the influence of Jesus's teaching and personality was so powerful in the generation after his death that the belief eventually crystallised that Jesus had actually survived or risen from death.

But that account does not fit the actual historical facts – namely, that the resurrection of Jesus was being preached well before any great attention was being paid by believers to what Jesus had been or had taught in his lifetime. Historically speaking, interest in the life and teaching of Jesus sprang from belief in his resurrection, not vice-versa. It was the resurrection that led to faith, not faith that led to the resurrection. So I cannot assent to any explanation or interpretation of the resurrection which has a tendency to explain it away like this, or deny its roots in history. I doubt in fact whether attempts at explanation of the resurrection are profitable at all. But affirmation is different: from the very beginning it has been the common Christian experience and conviction that Jesus *is* alive, risen from the dead, a present person and a living power.

You may recall that, in connection with the risen Christ, St Paul uses the phrase 'new creation', and the phrase continues to be used in our Christian preaching and theology. If we take it seriously what we are saying is that what happened in the resurrection of Jesus was of the same dimension as what happened in the original, primeval creation – in the creation of the world.

Creation does not submit to the order and regularities of the world: it ordains them. If it is true that in the resurrection of Jesus new creation appears, then it cannot be explained in terms of the regularities of the old. We must speak of *miracle* – and of miracle in the old-fashioned sense of the word as an unprecedented event which does not fit within, and cannot be expained by, the normalities and regularities of nature.

It may be that we must use the same word, and in the same sense, of certain other events, from the virgin birth onward, recorded in the gospels and the Acts of the Apostles. One must speak carefully here. Many thoughtful people find that the marvellous order of nature, and the beauties of splendours which appear within that order, are themselves powerful signs of the wisdom and care of God – much more powerful than occasional departures from order. They do not need miracles to show them *that* God is, or *what* God is.

With this point of view I largely agree. But consider this. In the fullness of time, at a particular moment and place within the old creation, God discloses himself. Since God is who he is, that disclosure will be distorted if mankind is bludgeoned or frightened into receiving it: it can be received undistorted only if it is received by faith.

But faith can be born only if there is first attention – or attention to that particular event or person or place where the disclosure actually is. Remember how in the story of the burning bush Moses is drawn aside by this phenomenon to wait and listen for what may be told him.

When Moses, musing in the desert, found
The thorn bush spiking up from the hot ground,
And saw the branches, on a sudden, bear
The crackling yellow barberries of fire,

He searched his learning and imagination
For any logical, neat explanation,
And turned to go, but turned again and stayed,
And faced the fire and knew it for his God.
                    (Norman Nicholson, 'The Burning Bush')[2]

Attention does not compel faith but it precedes faith.

How, I ask myself, was *attention* drawn to Jesus and to the story of Jesus as it was preached in the first generation – attention adequate to the birth of so profound a faith? One certainly cannot exclude the possibility of the miraculous – of events so distinct from the regularities of the old creation that they would draw attention to the particular figure and the particular story through which faith might receive the divine self-disclosure.

But this does not necessarily mean that Christians should be expecting or hoping for the miraculous today. For in twenty centuries Jesus and the story of Jesus have become embedded in our culture. We have so many things to draw our attention to that figure and that story, and to suggest that they are worth attending to: things as rich and various as King's College Chapel, Cambridge, the music of Bach and Handel, Michelangelo's Pieta, the example of St Francis and the work of Mother Teresa; the poetry of Blake and Hopkins and Eliot, and the glass of Chartres Cathedral; and a vast range of interpretative writing, from the gospels themselves to works of our own day. Of these things the first generation of Christians had nothing – nothing at all. It should be no surprise if we do not have the one thing which they had – the attention-drawing power of the miraculous. It does seem to me rather self-indulgent on our part to expect or claim that also.

To return to the resurrection. Those who believed did not immediately assert the identity between Jesus and God: that belief or doctrine emerged through years of continuing experience and reflection. But from the first, believers did (if I may put it like this) mention Jesus and God in the same breath. Jesus had been raised by God, sealed as God's own, exalted to God's right hand. To worship, trust and obey Jesus was to worship, trust and obey God.

We must remember two things. First, the God with whom Jesus is so directly and uniquely associated is no small God, no mere tribal or territorial deity, no member of a pantheon. In Jewish belief of that time God is One, the Almighty creator and Lord of heaven and earth, controller of the destiny of nations.

And the second thing we must remember is that the Jesus who is sealed by this God as his own is the *crucified* One. There is no suggestion that it is only Jesus the teacher or Jesus the healer who is God's own, or that the crucifixion was some kind of exception or violation of that unique relationship in which he stands to God. On the contrary it is Jesus Christ 'and him crucified' whom St Paul preaches, so that we might almost say (and St Paul almost says it) that all that is necessary to know about Jesus is that he was crucified in the flesh and raised by God.

So from the earliest days of Christianity, the creator and Lord of heaven and earth is uniquely associated with the weakness and nakedness of the suffering figure on the cross. I know this is a very inadequate way of stating the matter, but I think it will serve for now. 'The cross', said Luther, 'is the hiding place of the power of God.' And it seems to me that the paradox which this contains is still the great glory and the great difficulty of Christian belief.

I believe, along with all Christians, that God is God, that he is the author and sustainer of a universe infinitely vaster and more complex than our forbears had reason to believe. When I speak of God I must never forget what astronomers are detecting through their radio-telescopes and micro-physicists in their laboratories. I must never reduce or domesticate God to a dimension less awesome than that of the universe itself. I must never confine God within the limits of what satisfies *my* needs, *my* hopes or *my* imagination: on the other hand I believe, with all Christians, that 'God was in Christ reconciling the world to himself', and that the key place or point of reconciliation is the cross. I believe that what we see on the cross is not an interruption of *what* God is or a departure from *where* he is but the central point of a saving and reconciling self-disclosure to the world.

When I speak of God I must never forget the one lost sheep, the one human being in agony or despair; I must never forget the tears of one starving child. I must never sweep such things under the moral carpet; I must never think the world's tragedy is somehow necessary to God's grand design. It is these very things which must be reconciled, these situations which must be healed and saved, if God is truly God of a suffering world. We must never distance God so far from the world that he cannot know within himself its suffering, and cannot be exposed to share its grief. The divine crown is one of thorns.

The world has always been a place of suffering: but now, with wider possibilities of communication, we become ever more aware of the range and dimensions of its suffering. The problem of pain has become, for Christian believers, perhaps *the* problem of our age. I am certain that the problem is not to be met by increasingly unbelievable assertions by Christians that suffering, unacceptable though it is to us, is willed by God and therefore for the best.

I believe that we must assert, by the way we live as well as by what we teach, that suffering is never God's will but always his *burden* – a burden borne by God with no less agony and anguish than when Jesus bore his burden in Gethsemane, or when we must bear our loneliness and despair. 'Only the suffering God can help' (Bonhoeffer).[3] We must assert this; we must assert that God has not left us to drown alone in our own blood, sweat and tears – he too has cried the same tears and sweated the same blood.

But at the same time we must assert that he who shares so intimately the world's suffering is also the awesome and most holy author of the world's being, the God of the galaxies, the Alpha and Omega of time and space. Only, I think, if we can affirm both of these things can we make with credibility as well as with conviction the claim which I take to express the very heart of our faith – the claim that 'neither death, nor life, nor angels, nor principalities, nor things present, nor things to come, nor powers, nor height, nor depth, nor anything else in all creation, will be able to separate us from the love of God in Christ Jesus our Lord' (Rom. 8:38–9).

I want to add an appendix. The life of faith begins with an act of trust. As it goes on the evidence accumulates. We find we are living in God's world, and there are signs all around of his working, because we have the clue in the Lord of the cross. We often have to renew the act of trust.

The things which happen to us and the things which are demanded of us never compel us to acknowledge they are from God. But gradually our world is reorganised round Christ as its centre, and we have not the proofs we asked for at the beginning but an assurance which is held by faith and a hope which is stronger than man's proofs.

The Lord of the cross accepted as the word of salvation. That sounds jargon. But it does actually save. It saves from discouragement and despair – all the things that would otherwise discourage you become links that unite you with the Lord on the cross. It commits you to obedience and deals with your disobedience day by day. It saves you in death because death is the last unavoidable thing that unites you with Christ – and beyond it is his resurrection.

There are some people today anxious to speak as if belief were a great burden, and are anxious that no one shall escape without the full load. Let me assure you that the Christians who cope ultimately, I believe, and I have met a good many in the most testing circumstances in a great variety of cultures and countries, are people whose faith is cross and resurrection and not dogged, dull, demanding duty. When they condemn they only condemn the sins that their Lord condemned – hypocrisy, calculated worldliness and offences against the law of love.

I find the emancipated people human beings whose infectious faith seems not unbelievable but unquenchable. I want to belong to this company.

Notes

1. Christopher Bryant, *The Heart in Pilgrimage*. 1980.
2. Norman Nicholson, in *Five Rivers*. 1944.
3. Dietrich Bonhoeffer, *Letters and Papers from Prison*. 1953.

Encountering God: when belief fails*

In this chapter it is the turn of a Roman Catholic layman, Dr EAMON DUFFY, a Church historian and Fellow of Magdalene College, Cambridge, to look at the darker side of the Christian journey. He speaks in very personal terms of his own loss of faith following a devastating bereavement, and of the recovery of his belief that 'reality is to be trusted'.

We are supposed to live in an age in which belief is harder than ever before. In fact the Dean of Emmanuel College, Cambridge thinks that belief in any traditional form is just not possible for modern men and women.[1] According to him, humanity in the late twentieth century finds itself alone in a disenchanted universe, the age-old props and comforts of religion have fallen away, and we are left with an austere, demanding, individual task of imposing meaning on the inane, of making ourselves and our ideals the heart of a heartless world. If we choose to call these ideals God, well and good; but when we say we 'believe' in God we *do not* mean, the argument goes, what people in the past have meant by that. Their God was a sort of super-hero, a Dr Who figure, who made the lightning flash and the sun rise and who could be invoked to fend off the horrors of existence. This is superstition, says Don Cupitt, and so is any account of God which does not acknowledge that God is simply the sum of our human values, representing 'their ideal unity, their claims upon us and their creative power'. In other words; penetrate

* First published in *New Blackfriars* (May 1985).

to the heart of religion, look closely at the image in the shrine, and what you will find is not the unseen God, but a mirror. The true name of Yahweh is Narcissus. And we have heard this before. It is, with a change to a kindlier, less triumphalist tone, the voice of Victorian atheism:

> Is not this the great God of your sires, that with
>   souls and with bodies was fed,
> And the world was aflame with his fires? O fools,
>   he was God and is dead.
> Yea, weep to him, lift up your hands; be your eyes
>   as a fountain of tears;
> Where he stood there is nothing that stands; if he
>   calls there is no man that hears.
> Thou art smitten, thou God, thou art smitten; thy death
>   is upon thee, O Lord.
> And the love song of earth as thou diest resounds
>   through the wind of her wings –
> Glory to Man in the Highest! for Man is the Master
>   of things.
>
> (Swinburne, 'Hymn of Man')

But in any case the Church does not preach a God who is ever ready to bail us out of trouble, a general anaesthetic against the pain of being human. Such a God *would* be a superstition, and an unbelievable one too, since you only have to look around you to find pious Christians with cancer, or mangled in road-crashes. Christianity has never involved belief in a God of the gaps, a God who is the item of last resort in the medicine-cabinet of remedies for our human ills. God is presented to us in Christian tradition, not as an escape hatch *from* reality, but as the *ground* of reality, in whom we live and move and have our being. He does not, and never has, lived out there in a heaven that astronauts have proved does not exist, or as the end term in a sequence that philosophers now tell us need not have an end.

So what are we to make of this claim that *modern* men and women *cannot* believe in God? Patently millions of them do, not all of them intellectual primitives or young fogeys.

Perhaps the claim means that intelligent and sensitive modern people, as clued up on modern thought as the Dean of Emmanuel, cannot believe in the God of tradition. Again, I am not sure what to make of this, given that three of the philosophy chairs at Oxford and Cambridge are occupied by Roman Catholics of a rather traditional sort, and that one of Cambridge's most brilliant theoretical physicists recently resigned his chair to become an Anglican priest. So in what sense is 'modern' being used? I begin to suspect the presence of Humpty Dumpty.

> 'There's glory for you.'
> 'I don't know that you mean by glory,' Alice said.
> 'I mean there's a nice knock down argument for you.'
> 'But glory doesn't mean a nice knock down argument,'
> Alice objected.
> 'When I use a word,' said Humpty Dumpty in a rather scornful tone, 'it means just what I choose it to mean, neither more nor less.'

I find myself, then, a beachcomber along the edges of the sea of faith. I am to speak of unbelief, to try to pick from the flotsam and jetsam of my own experience some reflections on doubts about the existence of God, and the worth of religion. And what I want to register at the outset is my scepticism about the notion that it is somehow harder for us to believe because we *know* more, *understand* more, about the world than people in the past. Belief in God, in the God of Abraham and Isaac and Jacob, who acted in Jesus, who was before the worlds and will survive them, the God from whom we are born and into whom we die; belief in that God is not now, and never has been, a matter of a collection of opinions and ideas about the world. The saints and theologians and the simple believers of the past cannot be dismissed as a bunch of flat-earthers, whose God is some sort of discredited spiritual technology. Belief in God is now what it always has been, a matter of trust and reliance in the hopefulness and goodness of reality, and our place in it. Knowledge as such hardly affects it, and cannot in itself hinder or help it. Ask yourself;

who will find it harder to believe in a loving, caring, creator God – a secure western scientist in search of explanations in a warm laboratory, or a peasant woman in Ethiopia whose children have starved to death before her eyes? I want to suggest that it is not immediately obvious that the scientist will have the more strenuous task in believing. And accordingly I am unimpressed by the suggestion that the undoubted marginalising of religion in our society has much, or anything, to do with knowledge, or intellectual advance. I think that the explanation lies elsewhere. Since the onset of the Enlightenment, for at least three hundred years, we in the West have been systematically constructing a world in which men and women are dehumanised; pushed into anonymous multitudes, as 'hands' in the production of commodities, or as 'consumers' in an economy dominated, not by human needs, but by market forces. And within these collectivities they have been isolated, peddled an understanding of identity which is defined by separation from others, peddled an understanding of freedom as individualism. Our closest bonds are vested interest, or solidarity for the purpose of waging war. This is the dark side, the soft underbelly, of that process which the Dean of Emmanuel welcomes, by which 'in contemporary society scientific knowledge plays an ever-increasingly important part', offering 'a way of arriving at the truth which is very different from the traditional teaching of the Christian Church'. Indeed it is! That process seems to me to rest on the puerile assumption that one rule will do to measure all of reality, that all that cannot be quantified must be jettisoned. We strip our common discourse of all but utilitarian words and notions, and then greet the disappearance of non-utilitarian concerns and beliefs, firstly as somehow surprising, and then as somehow progress. We put out our eyes, and then insist that the sun is a fiction of the poets. But humanity is not by its nature the inhabitant of what D. H. Lawrence called 'the dry sterile little world the abstract mind inhabits'. The matter is essentially a simple one: empty society of the experience of shared value and commitment, exclude wonder and reverence as legitimate human responses to the world, isolate men and women within the trap of their own limited and limiting goals, and they will cease to speak of God. They will have forgotten his name, because they will not know their own.

> It was there that they asked us
> our captors, for songs,
> our oppressors, for joy.
> Sing to us, they said, one of Sion's songs.
> O how could we sing
> the song of the Lord
> on alien soil?   (Ps. 136)[2]

If there is any truth at all in the idea that we live in an age of *doubt*, it lies not in the advance of knowledge, but in the impoverishment of our collective perceptions, in the emptying of our language and our society of anything but number and calculation. Blake saw it coming, and denounced it at the beginning of the modern era.

> What, it will be questioned, when the sun rises, do you not see a round disc of fire somewhat like a guinea?
> O no, I see an innumerable company of the heavenly host crying HOLY HOLY HOLY is the Lord God Almighty.[3]

But of course lack of belief in God cannot just be explained away by social conditioning, any more than belief can. Doubt, the fear that the world has indeed no direction, that all man's aspirations are trivialised by death, the death of the individal or the generation or – a new possibility in our time – the species, the conviction that our goodness passes away and our evil can never be undone; these things touch all of us. If we are to be believers it cannot be by pretending that no one has these feelings or that they are not formidable and persuasive. It cannot be by pretending that we do not feel them ourselves.

I have no claim to expertise in these matters, and I have no illusion that my experience or perception of things has any sort of exemplary status. But in thinking about the failure of belief, I thought that the best thing I could do was to describe

26

my own failure of belief. Not the repeated infidelities, the hundred failures of commitment and conviction that seem to make the substance of my life as a Christian; but one particular period in my life when, quite simply, I became certain that there was no God, and that Christianity was an illusion.

I had my basic religious education from Irish monks, in the bad old days before the Second Vatican Council. It was a tough training, involving total saturation in Catholic subculture, 'God is Love' thumped into you with a stick and the penny catechism. You can do one of two things about the sort of conditioning that form of education gives you; you can kick against it and turn it on its head – like James Joyce – or wallow in it. I wallowed because I loved it. It provided me with a world of colour, historical resonance, poetry and intellectual vigour way beyond anything else in my provincial Irish upbringing. And when, as a teenager, I came to England, I was lucky enough to be sent to a school where religious education was in the hands of two exceptionally gifted men. At a time when most teenagers are quite understandably rejecting the threadbare platitudes that often pass for Christianity, I was being made to read Kafka and Sartre and Camus and Wittgenstein and Ryle, I was being introduced to the critical study of the Bible, I was being shown that religion had something worth hearing to say about all the issues of life and death. So I went to university, and read theology and philosophy, to begin with. And though I met and liked and talked through many long days and nights with people who did not believe, I never encountered anything that seemed half so rich or so satisfying as my inherited Catholicism. I married a Christian, and so never had to confront the problem of fundamental allegiance that being in love with a non-believer might have posed. Three years research in Church history only confirmed all this, and my satisfaction was bolstered by the willingness of many of the people I met to be influenced by me. I was not only religious, I was *successfully* religious. And all this in the 1960s, when the Church and the world were in such exciting ferment, when the worst idiocies of the Catholic Church seemed to be peeling

27

away, and when religous and political and social commitment
seemed to flow together; when one could spill out of a mass
at the chaplaincy, to take part in a silent demo in the market
place against napalm bombing in Vietnam. Heady days.

In my last year or so at Cambridge I was introduced to a
blind man, a retired Anglican priest, who lived just outside
Cambridge. I used to cycle out once a week to read to him.
He was a very remarkable person; despite his blindness he
edited a magazine, and was at the centre of an ever-expanding
circle of friends of every class, creed, colour, shape and sex –
he married a number of them off to each other! He was a life-
giver, full of wisdom, which he disguised with a rather
freakish, macabre sense of humour.

In 1971 I moved away to my first job, and I just about
kept in touch with him; and then in the following year I got
news, very unexpectedly, that he had died.

It turned out to be the most traumatic event of my life.
Never before or since has anything so terrible happened to
me. I still do not know why I was so affected, but in the
weeks after his death I woke up night after night, drenched
in icy sweat, swept by wave after wave of nauseating physical
fear of death; my own, my wife's, our new-born son's. Not
fear that somehow we might die *soon*, unexpectedly; just a
horrifying realisation that one day there would be nothing;
that our hopes, our preoccupations, our beliefs would be
simply brushed aside, shown up for the meaningless treadmill
they had always been. And with the horror, came the realisation that God was gone; there was no God, and I had no
faith. All the conditioning, all the arguments and emotional
scaffolding I had built round and into my life were as if they
had never been. I no longer believed, no longer even wanted
to believe; I was absolutely mesmerised by this overwhelming
perception of mortality. I had never been much good at
prayer, and now more than ever prayer seemed hollow. I felt
confused and embarrassed by my attempts to pray, like a
man caught talking to himself in a railway carriage.

What I want to emphasise is that *intellectually* nothing had
changed. The arguments for or against belief seemed neither
stronger nor weaker to me than they had ever done before; I

28

could still, and endlessly I *did*, put up a strong case for believing in God. Quite simply, it carried no weight for me. The death of my blind friend seemed the ultimate rebuttal. He was dead; everything, good or bad, would die.

I had encountered this awful annihilating blanket of death once before; but that had been safely between the covers of a book I had read as a sixth-former, Camus's *l'Etranger*. There is a horrifying scene towards the end of the novel, where the Outsider is waiting for execution in the death cell, and he explains the mystery which has dominated the book so far, his own total deadness of feeling, his inability to love or to hate, or to regret or to hope. A priest is trying to talk to him, and the Outsider, just for once, explodes.

> I hurled insults at him, I told him not to waste his rotten prayers on me; it was better to burn than to disappear . . . he seemed so cocksure, you see. And yet none of his certainties were worth one strand of a living woman's hair. It might look as if my hands were empty. Actually I was sure of myself, sure about everything, far surer than he. Sure of my present life and the death that was coming . . . all the time I'd been waiting for this present moment, for that dawn, tomorrow's or another day's, which was to justify me. Nothing had the least importance, and I knew quite well why. From the dark horizon of my future a sort of slow persistent breeze had been blowing towards me, all my life long, from the years that were to come. And on its way that breeze had levelled out all the ideas people tried to foist on me in the unreal years I was living through. What difference could they make to me, the death of others or a mother's love or his God . . . As a condemned man himself, couldn't he grasp what I meant by that dark wind blowing from my future?[4]

Now, standing in the full blast of that same dark wind, my plight had none of that appalling eloquence or clarity. But I felt myself confronted with the same issue. Were love and meaning to be flattened by my conviction that the world did not add up, that it had no significance greater than the sum

29

of its parts? If people were ephemeral, were the things they lived by and for ephemeral? Looking at what had been lovable and admirable in my friend's life, could I just say that had been 'nice' and turn away? Could I say, in fact, 'death is stronger than love'?

I found I could not, and the implications of my inability to say that baffled me. I could find no way of holding on to the values of Christianity while denying the account Christianity gave of reality. It would not do to say that, yes, the world *was* a bleak place subject to inexorable material forces, and yet that one might as well structure one's life by values like love and selflessness and compassion, because they were really very attractive. I did not see how righteousness could be reduced to some sort of pleasant and useful hobby like carpentry or crocheting, something to fill in the time till the hearse came to take me away. And I could not make any sense of the idea of defeated virtue for its own sake. I once saw an appalling newsreel of the Russian invasion of Hungary, in which a man rushed into the streets with a national flag which he brandished defiantly in the path of an oncoming tank, till it rolled over him with a noise like crackling sweet-papers. Was goodness like that; was *Jesus* like that? I found that I simply could not see righteousness as *pathetic*, a lost cause, like defeated Jacobite squires drinking to the king over the water who would never come into his own. I did not see how one could affirm the beatitudes, and yet assert that in no circumstances whatever would the meek inherit the earth.

All this time I had carried on going to mass, though I didn't know what I was doing there. And it was there, in its celebration of the death of Jesus (and what an extraordinary idea the *celebration* of a death seemed), that I found something by which I could establish some sort of bearing on my turmoil. For as I knelt there rather numbly, week by week, it dawned on me that the mass began from the point at which I had now arrived. Here, in a ritual grown commonplace to me by long aquaintance, there was an unblinking contemplation of all the ills of humanity. Here it was acknowledged that men and women die, often horribly, that good is defeated, that power crushes tenderness, that lies swallow up the truth. And in the face of that acknowledgement, in the face of the cross, the mass proclaimed a celebration, an affirmation of the unquenchable life of love. Out of death – and not just the death of Jesus, but out of *my* death, the masterful negation and collapse of all that made *me* man – it asserted our right to rejoice. It did so because there had once been a man whose trust in the loving reality that underlay the world was so total that in the face of his own destruction he could still call that reality Father; whose death was not an end to his loving, but the means of its infinite expansion. I saw that what was on offer here, true or false, was not an escape from my own mortality, for it began with a death. Karl Rahner says somewhere that 'when we look on the face of the Crucified we know that we are to be spared nothing'. What was on offer was an account of our living and dying which did justice to its urgency, and its fragility, and its lovableness; which affirmed that the forces that give warmth and worth to our existence have power in the dark places, even in death.

And I knew I had to choose, between the bleak valueless world of the Outsider and the world of human significance, where love and forgiveness and celebration were possibilities.

I do not have much recollection of the process by which I made my choice; except that, when it dawned on me that I had made it, it seemed not so much a choice as a gift. As I sat after communion one Sunday, simply looking at the people walking up to the altar, I was quietly overwhelmed with an overflowing sense of companionship, of gratitude, of joy and, oddly, of pity. My mind filled up, quite literally filled up, I could think nothing else, with a single verse of the Psalms (26:8):

Lord, how I love the beauty of your house,
and the place where your glory dwells.

There was no miraculous conviction. Perplexities and pain remained. I had and I have fewer certainties than before, and there are many areas of the faith that I gratefully and wholeheartedly accept which are opaque to me, like the idea of life after death. But now I know that faith is a direction, not a state of mind; states of mind change and veer about, but we can hold a direction. It is not in its essence a set of beliefs *about* anything, though it involves such beliefs. It is a loving and grateful openness to the gift of being. The difference between a believer and a non-believer is not that the believer has one more item in his mind, in his universe. It is that the believer is convinced that reality is to be trusted, that in spite of appearances the world is very good. When we respond to that good, we are not responding to something we have invented, or projected. Meaning is not at our beck and call, and neither is reality. When we try to talk *about* that reality we find ourselves talking *to* it, not in philosophy but in adoration, for it is inescapably personal, and most luminously itself in the life and death of Jesus. Christians are those who find in that life and death an abounding fountain of joy and hope and life; who affirm and are content to affirm what he affirmed about God, because they find in that affirmation a realism which does justice to life in all its horror and all its glory. Not sad, high-minded men with a handful of high-minded, bleak ideals, but citizens of a world whose heart is love. We know in the way of Jesus, not a *law*, but a liberation into true humanity; the power to love, to belong to one another, to start again when things go wrong, to be grateful, to adore.

Everyone of us, every human being, confronts at some time the collapse of meaning and direction in their lives – in anxiety, in illness, in unemployment or broken relationships, in all the forces that frustrate and diminish us as persons, and, at the last, in our own deaths. The Church has no pat answers to the dilemmas of existence, only a witness to what she knows. That under the mercy of God our perplexities, our failures, our betrayals, our limitations, can open into new freedoms, if we follow the way to Jesus. A century and a half ago Coleridge wrote:

Christianity is not a theory, or a speculation, but a Life; not a Philosophy of life, but a life, and a living Process . . . Try it.[5]

32

I don't know how to better that advice; like Coleridge I have found life in the God of Abraham and Isaac and Jacob, like millions of others in every age, like the psalmist before us:

I love the Lord, for he has heard
the cry of my appeal.
For he turned his ear to me
in the day when I called him.
They surrounded me, the snares of death,
with the anguish of the tomb:
They caught me, sorrow and distress:
I called on the Lord's name . . .
Turn back, my soul, to your rest
for the Lord has been good.
He has kept my soul from death,
my eyes from tears,
and my feet from stumbling.
I will walk in the presence of the Lord,
in the land of the living.   (Ps. 114)[6]

Notes

1. Don Cupitt, *The Sea of Faith*. 1984.
2. Grail Psalter.
3. William Blake, 'A Descriptive Catalogue', in *Works*, ed. Geoffrey Keynes. 1935.
4. Albert Camus, *The Outsider*. 1946.
5. S. T. Coleridge, 'Aphorism Seven', in *Aids to Reflection*. 1884.
6. Grail Psalter.

4

Encountering myself: guilt and forgiveness

The Archbishop of Canterbury speaks in Chapter 1 of our need to be 'unconditionally accepted and totally loved'. The Roman Catholic writer and consultant psychiatrist Dr JACK DOMINIAN takes up this theme. Turning from 'encountering God' to 'encountering myself', he explores the development in the earliest years of life of our sense of 'good' and 'bad'. He defines the origins of love, hate and guilt, and the healing which follows as we learn to forgive ourselves and gain 'our adult and mature freedom'.

There are certain experiences that permeate throughout humanity. One of these is the feeling of good and bad. In religious terms we refer to the notion of sin, but the consequences of sin are translated into the way we feel about ourselves, our thoughts and our actions. Everybody has a sense of right and wrong, which for the Christian ultimately becomes an encounter with or against God.

In this chapter I want to trace how the sense of good and bad arises in our personality, what are the consequences and how it can become distorted. There are those who believe that we are born bad, but that is not the Christian message. We are in fact created in the image of God, and our basic propensity is to reflect the majesty and fullness of this image. But we also know that humanity cannot achieve this. There is within men and women an inclination for negating goodness which is called original sin. Paul captures this when he says in Romans 7:15, 'I cannot understand my own behaviour. I fail to carry out the things I want to do, and I find myself doing the very things I hate'. A little later he adds, 'for though the will to do what is good is in me, the performance is not, with the result that instead of doing the good things I want to do I carry out the sinful things I do not want. When I act against my will, then it is not my true self doing it, but sin which lives in me'. Paul is speaking here as an adult, but my task is to try and trace how this conflict, which he describes, arises.

In order to do this we must retrace our steps and go back to the early years of life. Most of us have forgotten our first half a dozen years, but it is during this time that the origins of love and hate occur. In using the words 'love' and 'hate' I have already indicated that the basic encounter in human life is about love. It is about love of self and neighbour. I need not remind you that in the Judaeo-Christian tradition we find in this love of man and of God the basic commandments of holiness. In the First Epistle of John (4:11–12) we are told: 'My dear people, since God has loved us so much, we too should love one another. No one has ever seen God; but as long as we love one another God will live in us and his love will be complete in us.' Thus at the heart of the encounter with ourselves and with others lies the capacity to love.

But how does love develop? We start life as an act of love and some nine months later we are born. Throughout pregnancy the mother establishes a relationship with the foetus, and after the birth there develop a series of emotional experiences which constitute what we understand by love. Let us look at these.

The first thing that happens, according to John Bowlby, is that the infant forms an attachment to its mother. It learns within days to relate to her by making an affectionate bond. This bond is mediated through sight – the mother is recognised; through sound – her voice becomes familiar; through touch which gives the sense of safety; and through smell. In this way we learn to recognise and be recognised as a significant person. The beginnings of personhood and interpersonal encounter are laid down. Within this attachment, this bond, which is the foundation of love, other characteristics of love will be added little by little.

35

Within the first year of life as babies we experience physical care. We are fed, washed, played with, and learn the sensation of being held safely, of warmth and comfort. According to E. Erikson, these activities, which are all physical, give us the sense of trust. We learn as babies that we can be squeezed and not smothered, held and lifted and not dropped. Although we do not remember these events we can recognise them later on when we are a little older and indeed we repeat them with those we love in adult life. At first trust is physical, but in the years that are to follow this trust will be extended into words, and we learn to trust what our parents say. In this way parents become trustworthy and we gradually acquire that sense ourselves; we learn to trust our own experiences.

This is the beginning of love of self. Gradually we begin to trust ourselves, that is to say, to possess ourselves. At the heart of love of self is the ability to own our bodies, feelings and mind. This sense of self-acceptance is vital because, if we do not own ourselves, we cannot donate the self to others. We cannot give what we do not possess. Psychiatrists see many people who are precisely in this state, men and women who feel useless and cannot believe they have anything to offer to others.

So in these early years the encounter with parents facilitates the sense of owning our lives. Nevertheless, at this time we are still weak, powerless and totally dependent for survival on our parents.

What happens next is of vital importance. In the second and third year of life we acquire an enormous repertoire of autonomy. We learn to crawl, stand up, and walk. We learn to feed and dress ourselves and to speak. This is an enormous extension of capabilities and indeed no other phase in our life will show such growth. Since growth in childhood is the process of gradual separation between ourselves and our parents over a period of some twenty years, these and subsequent years are the beginning of our self-sufficiency. Now here we come to a fundamental psychological moment. We are learning to become independent, to own our bodies, feelings and mind, but we need not only to own them but to feel what we own is good. We depend on our parents to give us the sense of goodness which is attached to every aspect of our development. In this way we feel good when we walk, dress, feed, talk, and later on when we have thoughts, opinions and want to express our feelings. This process by which our growth is blessed with a sense of goodness is vital to our love of self. We now feel not only that we own our bodies, feelings and minds, but furthermore that what we own is good.

Once again psychiatrists and others meet men and women who feel both empty, useless and impotent, and no good. Such people have grown up with a sense of being unwanted, ignored, unappreciated, criticised. They were neither granted their independence nor affirmed in the possession of themselves. They continue to remain dependent on authority, they feel incomplete and useless because they lack a sense of owning themselves and the feeling that what they own is good. Such self-rejecting emptiness can be contrasted with Christ's certainty of himself. In John's Gospel we read (8:14), 'It is true that I am testifying on my own behalf, but my testimony is still valid, because I know where I came from and where I am going.' And again he asserts his goodness (10:14), 'I am the good shepherd'. And finally the certainty of his relationship with his father, 'You must believe me when I say that I am in the Father and the Father is in me' (14:11). In contrast to human uncertainty Christ shows a certainty of ownership and goodness which suggests that his was the perfect upbringing of love.

Those who cannot separate themselves from their parents learn to equate dependence on others as the holiness of obedience. Christianity has built false theories of holiness, and one of them has been to make obedience to authority a counsel of excellence. It is, of course, nothing of the sort. Christ's obedience to his Father was not an expression of immature obedience but an adult commitment of free choice. Even more important, if we do not own ourselves, if we have no love of self, we have little or nothing to offer to others or to love them with. Our love of others depends on the gradual enlargement of ourselves through twenty years of life. The more of ourselves we possess, in a positive and affirmative manner, the more we can love others. The greatest lover of all was Christ because, having possessed himself completely, he could give himself totally to others. Most of us are in the process of discovering and possessing ourselves throughout our lives, and this process of liberation from parents, figures of authority, teachers and others, is part of our unending maturation. If we do not possess ourselves we continue to live our lives by kind permission of others, our parents, teachers, our spouse and the Church. The trouble is that such dependence on others is often accompanied by deep frustration, resentment and a continuous desire to rebel.

One final point about self-acceptance. If we grow up feeling unwanted, rejected, of little value, we have a tendency to seek as our intimate friends those who criticise and put us down. Like moths we seek the lamp and we get burned. We grow up conditioned to self-rejection and we do not know what to do with acceptance and appreciation. We have a poor opinion of ourselves and we surround ourselves with those who respond in a similar manner. Such people turn to God in the hope that they will find acceptance there. It is true that God's love is unconditional, but psychologically it is even truer that if we cannot experience acceptance horizontally from our neighbour we will find it very difficult to receive it vertically from God.

Having clarified one psychological principle, namely, that of self-possession and self-esteem, we return to the second and third year of life to consider another psychological dimension. We can imagine the child learning to do things for itself, feed and dress itself, crawl and walk. Each of these processes is surrounded with mess, the trial and error process. If we watch a child feed itself at that age, some food goes into the mouth and much on the floor. Learning to fasten one's buttons is a confusing issue. Standing up and exploring the world means that precious objects are broken. In all processes of learning the child is vulnerable and dependent on the goodwill of the parent. Patience, tolerance, understanding are not the prerogative of all parents who easily exhaust them. All goodwill has its limits and at some point father or mother shouts and smacks. The child experiences this as a profound shock.

The source of all love is angry and has shown aggressive tendencies. Children feel bad for upsetting the parent, and this sense of badness is accompanied by feelings of guilt. The child blames itself for what has happened. It has no knowledge of parental limitation. It feels bad through and through and for a moment is saturated with badness and guilt. All this is momentary. The parent reaches out and makes it up. The child feels forgiven, guilt disappears and love is restored. That is the usual process of reconciliation which goes on throughout childhood. But there are immense dangers in this exchange.

At the heart of the exchange just described is the child's feelings of badness and guilt because it has displeased the parent. I am now about to point out the second experience of badness in our life. The first was the sense of lacking affirmative possession of ourselves, the second is when we feel bad because we have displeased those who love us. The most common experience of human guilt is because we feel we have hurt someone who loves us. But in our childhood the sense of badness and guilt is total, and we are completely dependent on the goodwill of our parents to rescue us from this state. Most of us gradually learn that our parents are not perfect and our sense of badness and guilt becomes less than total, lessens as we learn that it is not entirely our fault, that some of the responsibility lies in the limitations of our parents.

Some people, however, grow up without this process of maturation. Whenever they hurt those they love, however slightly, they experience an exaggerated sense of badness and guilt and cannot forgive themselves. These men and women grow up with parents who perpetrated the sense of guilt and badness in them. Parents who were extremely sensitive, could not feel responsible and made their children bear the responsibility for all their limitations. The same applies to those who could not easily forgive or accept apology from their children. We meet such people who are so sensitive that the slightest criticism sends them into a massive huff. As parents they exact the same sense of guilt from their children. The tragedy of this upbringing is that such children continue to feel totally bad and have a profound sense of guilt instilled into them at a time when they were not free to know any better and they go on perpetuating these feelings later on in life.

I can sum up what I have said so far by saying that at the heart of love is to be found self-acceptance and self-esteem, which allows us to love others as ourselves, and that one sense of badness and guilt is the inability to do this. The other sense of badness and guilt is denied when we hurt those we love, and this is the most fundamental experience of badness.

Two objections can be raised at once to what I have said. First, that I have given so much responsibility to our parents that we could draw the conclusion that it is all their fault and as a consequence we never need to feel guilty about our conduct. Not so. Our conduct is our responsibility. What I am suggesting is that first we have to expel negative parental influences so that we reach a degree of freedom from which we can truly make free choices. Our badness and our guilt must be truly ours, and not an expression of what our parents and teachers had instilled in us. Only then can our blame, guilt and self-forgiveness belong authentically to us.

The second objection is far more important. I have made the key of human badness dependent on the capacity or incapacity to love, but that is not the usual understanding of badness. The more common interpretation is that ultimately all our badness stems from our selfishness. In Freudian terms, the infant is seen as a seething mass of pleasure-seeking and aggression. Its basic intent is gratification of both, and its earliest experiences are narcissistic, self-gratifying. Gradually this principle of pleasure gives way to reality which in the form of our parents, teachers and morality forbid both the gratification of instincts and the expression of aggression.

Life thereafter is a battle between the suppression and the realisation of instincts. It never ceases to surprise me how Freud the atheist and Christianity share this vision of man as a selfish, self-centred, instinctive brute eager to unleash his sexuality and aggression. Hence all of us have been conditioned to feel badness and guilt when our instincts and aggression are allowed free rein. The commonest basis of all Christian morality has been the control of self and the accompanying guilt feelings when we want to indulge

40

ourselves. Pathetically all too commonly the moral strictures of Christianity have been limited to the avoidance of sex and aggression.

But primarily I do not see Christ in this summary of the law. The summary of the law was to love God and our neighbour as ourself. It is not surprising that Christianity in the West is in such doldrums when the basic teaching of Christ is ignored. Our only aim in life must be to feel bad only when we fail to love God, self and our neighbour. This is recognisable Christianity. This is recognisable biblical theology.

And so I turn to that part of psychology which is concerned with the growth of love. It is called neo-Freudian and it is the work of such people as Horney, Fromm, Sullivan, Winnicot, Bowlby, Erikson. In it will be found the personal encounter between child and parent as the foundation of love in our first intimate experience of life. This love is repeated in subsequent intimate experiences with our friends, spouses and God. In these subsequent experiences we have the opportunity to heal our wounds contracted in our first intimate experience.

Spouses and friends heal us by giving us a second opportunity to do two things. First they give us the experience of unconditional love. They accept us with our faults and limitations, and they begin to make us feel lovable simply because we are. We do not have to earn our love, we do not have to do things in order to be appreciated. We are simply loved because we exist, which is precisely the ideal parental love. This is exactly the love that Christ offered to the sinner. The prostitute, the tax collector, were all accepted unconditionally because they accepted Christ, the source of all love. Christ's only conditions were to have faith in him and to *change in the heart*. This metanoia simply asks that we believe in love, and it is in this spirit that we put ourselves into the hands of others who love us. What we want first is unconditional acceptance, the removal of rejection. If we feel accepted, we can begin to accept ourselves.

The second thing that those who love us give to us is the opportunity to learn how to love them. Previously all we have known is to please out of fear, duty or the sense of guilt. In

41

other words, our love has been no more than compliance to power. But St John tells us that we cannot love if we fear. And so our friends and spouses give us room to find our freedom initially and begin to love because we want to do so. Christ asked for the heart of faith, a freely chosen love no longer coloured by fear or guilt. His love of his Father was a total free commitment and that is what he wants from us. So healing goes on throughout our lives in friendship, marriage, and in our relationship with God in and through prayer and the sacraments.

But does all this mean that badness has been eliminated? Not at all, but the badness we have to encounter is not the rejection of ourselves. Rejection of ourselves is allied to despair and death, and some five thousand people kill themselves every year in England and Wales in that state. Many more do not kill themselves, but live without hope in the grips of self-rejection. The majority give up altogether and try to escape from acknowledging any feelings of goodness and badness. These are the people who have nominally left religion. But in fact no one can escape from the grips of loving. We can suppress sex and aggression, but every minute of our encounter with another human being is a test of love or alienation. We are with or against people. We love or we do not. Christ's message of life, death and resurrection was about the kingdom of God which is love.

And so our badness is not to be found primarily in our instincts or in our obedience to authority. Our goodness is not to be found in being good boys or girls. Our badness and goodness are to be found in our ability to love. That means freeing ourselves from childhood fears and guilt, gaining our adult and mature freedom, and then loving. Our badness reflects the extent to which we give up the struggle to become free to love. As far as loving is concerned, there is no limit of how far we can go. The gospels define the limits of love in the thought, word and action of Jesus Christ. We can never imitate him completely, but our Christian life is about being Christ-like.

Our goodness and badness are about being Christ-like. We can never love enough, and to that extent we are always failing. But this is not a failure of badness or wickedness. In and through our baptism we have become Christ-like, co-opted children of God. We have put on a new mantle, a new life. This reality is the capacity to love, and we no longer judge our badness but the measure of our love.

In a sense we can never forgive ourselves completely because that will happen eschatologically when we are united with the Trinity. But in forgiving ourselves continuously we do not confirm the guilt of our badness but the failure to love enough. I conclude with Augustine, who said, 'Love and do what you will.'

5

Encountering others: the politics of belief

'Encountering others' is the theme of the next two chapters. Dr COLIN MORRIS, Head of Religious Broadcasting at the BBC and one-time President of the Methodist Conference, spells out the implications of the Word made flesh. 'Once I start upon the way of Jesus all my encounters are thereby transformed.'

Part of the title I have been given talks about the politics of belief. Now I am not quite sure what that means, but I presume what it means is: what I believe, and its consequences for my attitudes to others. I guess that in a few pages you would not expect me to construct a system of Christian ethics. And therefore I must talk about foundational things: quite fundamental things that I believe and which, as a consequence, affect the way I behave in the world of persons.

I want to begin with *conversion*. Ah! they say. Has the old radical gone soft in the head in his declining years? It is very interesting, the way in which the word 'conversion' is greeted by looks of intense embarrassment in whole sections of the modern Church, because it is redolent of a sort of image of quivering-nosed fanatics, exuding super-heated piety, dashing around the place clapping people on the back and enquiring whether they are saved or not. And it is curious that there should be this reaction because conversion is a process which goes on in many, many areas of society. People are being converted to and from things all the time; and indeed there are certain personalities in many walks of life about whom it is impossible to be neutral. Once you have met them, you

44

can love them or you can hate them. But you will never be the same again.

And so when I talk about conversion being the point from which it begins I am not talking about self-indulgent soul-tickling. I am talking about a clear-eyed decision to walk *that* way, the way of Jesus, rather than another way; to do it as an act of will, and to do it in such a way that as a long-term consequence there will be in me a character change. The acid test of the genuineness of my conversion, I would submit, is not that it produces a kind of world-denying religiosity, which is more repellent than attractive, but that it affects the pressure-points of my life.

In the first place, it is not so much what it does to my church-going or to my hymn-singing but what it does to my attitudes to sex and money and ambition, and power and justice and race; in other words, the manifold activities where I encounter others. So I believe that the whole thing begins from a determination that I shall make my priorities the priorities of Jesus, and that I shall draw my power for living from the same source from which he drew his – that once I start upon the way of Jesus all my encounters are thereby transformed.

Now I suppose there are hundreds of ways in which I could characterise the impact upon me of the person and work of Jesus, and its impact upon the way in which I behave in the world of persons. I want to take, almost arbitrarily, one particular scheme and say that, first of all, it has to do with *the way in which I look upon others through the eyes of Jesus*; and then, in the second place, *the way in which I look for Jesus in others*. If I am talking about looking through the eyes of Jesus I suppose the classic proof-text is that word of Paul's about 'having in you the mind that was in Christ Jesus'(see 1 Cor. 2:16). And if you ask yourself what were the characteristics of the mind of Jesus, there are two in particular that it seems to me are quite crucial.

The first is that it was a mind that was massively concerned with specifics rather than universals. When those Greeks came to Jerusalem for the Passover, and they inquired of Philip whether they could meet Jesus, they would have been greatly disappointed had they expected to meet someone whom they regarded as a philosopher according to their culture, because by no standard would Jesus have been so qualified. He had no interest in speculation, he was not concerned with questions like, 'What would happen if . . .?' or 'Let us suppose that . . .' He was a man with a burning obsession. His spiritual and mental energy was not diversified into the business of bringing light in whole areas of human ignorance. It was a burning obsession with the kingly rule of God – not as an academic thesis, but as promise and as presence and as judgment in the midst of life.

Now if we consider how deep the roots of the doctrine of the kingly rule of God go in the history of the Jewish people, and then look at the way Jesus dealt with it, what is quite fascinating is how parochial he was. He did not prognosticate in terms of sweeping world views – which is why we get very embarrassed these days when we are required as a Church very often to say, Now, what would Jesus have said about the nuclear debate, unemployment, monetarism, bimetallism, you name it? And the truth is that he showed a massive lack of interest in many of these issues, so that we find ourselves piously sucking our thumbs to find anything that we can actually link on to what he said.

He had the audacity to claim that the secret of the kingly rule of God was to be found in a sample series of encounters with people who, according to the parables, were not particularly virtuous, did not make any particularly profound statements, and did not do anything particularly heroic. And yet he said, in those encounters – with an unscrupulous steward, with a crafty businessman, with a busy housewife, with a farmer – somewhere in there, in those concrete actualities of daily encounter, was to be found the secret of the kingdom. Now you cannot get more parochial than that. You cannot get more specific than that. He said the secret of the kingdom was to be found not in the upper reaches of the universe but on the lower floors of the factory. It is not in the metaphysics of life; it is somewhere in the mechanics of it. It is not hidden away in the sayings of the sages; it is revealed nakedly in the eyes of the person next door. There is something in the very

46

specific that indicates the depth of something that it is impossible to specify; there is something at arm's length that testifies
to the unreachable.

This is one of the reasons why I suppose my thinking has
undergone something of a sea-change. I fear the universalism
of a Christian response to every issue under the sun. I fear
this 'Christianity and . . .', this 'conjunctional' Christianity
which says that we shall have something to say about everything. I fear many of those church pronouncements that turn
people into issues. I used to be the British Olympics Resol-
ution Composer and Proposer of the Methodist Church. I
fear text-books of systematic theology, which take the sayings
of this apocalyptic prophet and spin them out into majestic
syllogisms: neat, tidy, splendid. Because, you see, the secret
of the kingdom is not there.

One of the oldest Christian heresies is gnosticism. And it
is interesting how the old heresy keeps creeping back into the
Church in the desire for universal, disembodied perfection,
and in the desire to turn our backs upon the specific and the
concrete and the fleshly. I find it welling up in me when I
have to prepare addresses, and the neater they get, and the
more schematic, the more I get away from this sense of raw
reality.

There's the gnosticism of the religious broadcaster – this is
our creed: we are the great gnostics of the twentieth century.
We take flesh and blood, and we put them in front of a
microphone, and what issues out of the other end is words,
disembodied words. Or we take flesh and put it in front of a
camera, and what issues out of the other end is a disembodied
image. We reverse the incarnation – regularly, ten times a
day. Classic gnosticism! Which is why I find I have got to
concentrate, almost desperately, on a small number of actual,
living, breathing, human beings, if I am going to latch on, in
any way, to the 'Jesus thing'.

The other characteristic of the mind of Jesus, which seems
to me to be very relevant to this business of encountering
others, is the fact that he had a *'crucified rather than a crusading
mind'*.[1] The term is Kosuke Koyama's, who, being Japanese,
was at the receiving end of the triumphalist tradition of the

British – and not just of the British, but of the western missionary enterprise – someone who was accustomed to being at the receiving end of the 'crusading mind'. The cocksureness of the western missionary enterprise, the spiritual imperialism of it, the determination to know what was best for other people, the ability to take millions of unique human beings, and classify and label and dismiss them in one phrase – 'godless', 'heathen', 'pagan' – as neatly as that!

The 'crucified mind', on the other hand, is diffident, to the point of timidity; it is a mind that is conscious of the mystery of the other person, that recognises the sovereignty of the rights of another person, of the authenticity of their inner suffering, and is very careful about making judgments.

The crusading mind systematises, and therefore talks about Communism and Fascism and racism and humanism, and in so doing is able very neatly to turn mysterious human beings, untidy realities, into bodies of ideas and dispose of them. The crucified mind recognises that, though Communism for instance, does not live and love and bleed and die, Communists do. And therefore there is the possibility of encounter with other human beings, which can enrich both.

I think this is the secret of the sensitivity of Jesus. It is fascinating to recall the instance where he is surrounded by an absolute crowd of people crushing in on him, and he suddenly says, 'Who touched me?' because someone had touched the hem of his robe. Which gives a clue to this strange question: why does Jesus in the gospels not make a uniform demand upon people? Why does he make a variety of claims on them? Why is it that, in some instances, he meets an immediate need, and that is the end of it (as far as we know)? He gives sight to Bartimaeus, he raises from the dead Jairus's daughter, he heals the epileptic boy – and that is the end of it. As far as we are aware he makes no other claim upon them; they go their way. In another instance his demand is radical. He says: 'Sell all you have'; or, 'Give up everything'.

The crusading mind is quite imperious in its demand. Even evangelically it will say, 'all have heard, all who asked have received, therefore all shall obey.' And the same claim is laid upon all. The crucified mind recognises that there are those who will carry the cross to the end, and there are those who will lay it down through sheer weakness; it recognises that some people who say, 'Lord, Lord', will not live to the limit of their confession. Some people will bury their talent in the field, and others will put it to work.

Somewhere Arnold Toynbee talks about the Aeschylean clue to human history. Taken from Greek tragedy, this is the notion that all true learning comes from suffering – taken up, of course, by the author of the Epistle to the Hebrews, when he says that Jesus 'learned obedience through the things that he suffered'(5:8). The evolution of the crucified mind comes about because of a willingness to accept all the pain of human encounter, all its bane and blessing, all its joy and misery; to regret none of it except that which is futile, and to repent of none of it other than that which is sinful. And it is that kind of mind that characterises the Christian encounter with others.

Now if that is one end of the balance – the way in which you look through the eyes of Jesus at others – what about the other side of it? What about *looking for Jesus in others?* That, of course, takes us straight into the foundational doctrine of incarnation, the basic statement that the Word became flesh. It is a short phrase that preoccupies me, tantalises me, often drives me into a frenzy; but at the end of the day, it seems to me, it is absolutely central to any understanding of encountering others: talking about the way in which all that can be known of God in history is expressed through the limitations and the mysteries of human personality. In other words, God communicated himself through human encounter. The Christian response to this preoccupying question of all religions: 'How does God address humanity?' is not through the spirits of mountains and rivers and streams, as some say, or through an inerrant book that drops from heaven into the lap of one Joseph Smith, or through the conformation of the heavens, or through the voice of Auntie Aggie in the great Beyond, but *Truth investing personality.* This is the kind of truth that is of supreme significance. A textbook of child-care is of very little use to an orphan: he needs a mother. A medical dictionary is of marginal value to the seriously ill: they need

49

the touch of a doctor or nurse. No doctrine of salvation can take anybody out of a prison of self-preoccupation: they need a Saviour. Truth invested in human personality. Which is why, in so far as I have answers to those questions which preoccupy many human beings about God, I find at least the beginnings of an answer to be found in others.

How can I know God? I cannot, because God is not accessible to the human senses. But I can see Jesus at work through others. Does God care? Behold Jesus at work through others – healing, teaching, saving a lost world. For me this is absolutely central to my understanding of faith: the notion of Truth investing personality. This is the way God communicates. And also the notion of God and the world, Word and flesh, God and the world: you cannot have one without the other. You cannot have God without the world, as some pietists think. You cannot remake the world without God, as some secular idealists would love to do. If you want one, you must have the other. God without the world is an enigmatic abstraction. The world without God is a terrifying fiction.

'Who does this world belong to?' is a very interesting question. A lot of pietists say, 'The world belongs to God; keep well clear of it.' Others say, from their reading of history, 'The world belongs to whoever is strong enough to dominate it; so accept the inevitable.' The New Testament says, 'The world belongs to God; so get in there and claim it.' Very often we are accused, in the Church, of interfering in what is called politics. And maybe we have not made it sufficiently clear that we have no option; that because the Word has become flesh, we have got to go to the places where flesh is being bruised and tortured and starved *in order to find Christ*.

In the course of a not uneventful life, if I ask myself, 'What have I known most clearly about God?', and I give myself the truth drug, I get answers like this. If I ask, 'Where have I seen the purity of God?' I would have to say, 'On the face of a nun working in a slum in Latin America, trying to bring some dignity and wholesomeness under conditions which could legitimately be called hellish.' That is where I have seen God's purity: in a work which is a living parable of that tremendous truth in John's Gospel about there being a Light that no darkness can extinguish. If I personally have known the peace of God, I must confess it has not normally been in a church. But when I have attempted, however pathetically, however much in a restricted setting, to do a deed of reconciliation between races in Africa, I know that I have seen the righteousness of God in some very, very strange places, where prisoners of conscience languish behind bars or barbed wire because they will not bow the knee to Baal.

I often find myself echoing Moses' request to God that I might have a vision, just a flash, just a quick glimpse, or even just one syllable of a heavenly voice to encourage me as I plough my way through these wilderness years, where there is nothing to be seen but sun and sand and distance. I always seem to get the same response that Moses got: God says, 'No, I won't show you my face. But I'll show you my back.' I have seen God's back. I have seen God's back at a frontier-post in Africa, where a crowd of refugees have been on the very brink of safety and have then been turned back; and as they slouched off into the distance, and I looked at their backs, I was looking at the back of God.

Although I have spent a lot of my time in houses of God, I have a very clear recollection of an occasion in a tenement in the East End of London, when I was minister of Wesley's Chapel, on a day when, in this crowded tenement with water running down the walls, I suddenly had the extraordinary sense that I was a guest in the house of God – because racked human flesh was preaching an anguished word to me.

People often claim that the church is irrelevant. That is true when the Word does not become 'flesh-in-it'. The Word may have been transformed into splendid architecture, magnificent music, beautiful surroundings, but it has not become flesh. And if sometimes our prayers echo hollowly around places like that it may be that is because they remain words; they do not become flesh.

There are some well-meaning Christians who want to turn Christianity into a private transaction between the human soul and God. They want to get the Church out of this messy and very ambiguous encounter with a sad, bad world. They do not realise what they are trying to do. They are trying to reverse the incarnation. You can accept the Word-become-flesh; you may reject it; you may spurn it; you may even crucify it; and the purpose of God can still be accomplished. But if you re-spiritualise it you destroy the whole of Christianity. Because it was a *man* who laughed and bled and sweated, who died. So you cannot have God and avoid human encounter, because there is nowhere you can look where you will find him.

But I think the Word-become-flesh is also quite extraordinary endorsement about the world of persons, because it talks about the dependence of God, which seems to me to be unique to Christianity. The Word, Almighty Power, becomes flesh – this thing, which is weak and fallible and pathetic. Now Christianity shares many truths with other great religions. But this notion is unique. Where other faiths – quite properly – emphasise human dependence upon God, Christianity dares to talk about God's dependence upon humanity.

Was it not historically true? Did Jesus not need a human womb in which to be born, a human breast at which to suck, a human father to take him away to Egypt, away from Herod's wrath? Human friends to love and care – and betray him, a conscript to help carry the cross, someone, something to roll away the stone at the entrance to the tomb? Is it not historically true, God's need of people like us?

Is it not functionally true? Is it not true that he needs human hands to wield the instruments through which healing is done, and human eyes to look in compassion on the outcast, and a human presence to stand by the lonely, and human brain-power to make deserts fertile and feed the hungry? And human political skills to fight for a just and a humane social order? Is is not functionally true?

When people say, 'O God, do this, do that, do the other', by what agency do they imagine that this will be done? Bolts of lightning? Magical interference with the natural order? If God has supernatural agents and ministers of his grace they are opaque to human eyes. All we can say is that somewhere there is a human spirit and a human heart that is prepared to incarnate his will and purpose in a given place at a given time. I find that truth humbling and immensely dignifying, because it seems to me that this is a tremendous vote of confidence. It is a quite extraordinary act of faith – not our faith in God (our faith in God waxes and wanes this way and that) – but of God's faith in us, such that he is prepared to commit himself into treacherous hands like these; that he is prepared to make a cosmic wager, to take a chance that we will not let him down.

Now that is a one-sided truth, the notion of God's dependence upon us. But it is a truth which redeems any life from mediocrity, and it is a truth that invests every human encounter with a quite remarkable significance. But it seems to me that the pay-off line is that, just as the Word had to become flesh under Pontius Pilate in order that the world might be saved, unless the Word becomes flesh in people like us the world will not know that it *has* been saved. It will not know the things that belong to its peace.

Note

1. Kosuke Koyama, *Waterbuffalo Theology*. 1974.

6

Encountering others: working together

Liverpool, scene of great social deprivation, is also the scene of the most remarkable ecumenical leadership in this country, not least in the Churches' united and vigorous stand on social issues. DEREK WORLOCK, its Roman Catholic Archbishop, and DAVID SHEPPARD, its Anglican Bishop, further flesh out the theme that encountering others is inseparable from encountering God. They speak of the transformation which can follow from the recognition of our common baptism.

I. Bishop David Sheppard

Archbishop Derek Worlock and I are trying to learn a new skill; we have shared a pulpit a good many times; now we feel it best to try to write one chapter, but in four points.

We know that some people think we can be such close allies because we have a common mind about the great social needs of Liverpool. They assume that we by-pass all the religious stuff, and that this is why we have been invited to write not on 'Encountering God', but on 'Encountering Others'.

It is a great misunderstanding to pose these as opposites; to assume that because we speak out about unemployment and race relations we are not very interested in prayer. If people say that, how do they think they know? I know that this division between 'practical Christianity' and 'believing and praying Christianity' has been made for centuries. A local councillor, long since gathered to his fathers, accepted an invitation to the AGM of an East London settlement. He said he would not have come if it had been an ordinary church; but they stood for 'practical Christianity' and he was glad to support them.

Encountering others is not separate for a Christian from encountering God. The motivation to love your neighbour springs from that encounter with God.

I sat in Great St Mary's, Cambridge as a freshman thirty-five years ago: I had few connections with the Church; I believed in God in that unsatisfactory sense of agreeing to the Christian faith, faith in a God who seemed far distant from my everyday life. I did not agree with several things said by the preacher: yet somehow a whole tangle of loose threads started to come together. I went away with my friend who had invited me to come, and we talked late. Alone in my room that night I prayed as I had never prayed before. I realised that faith was not just assenting to some historic beliefs or moral code. It was about opening the whole of me to this living Lord. I prayed and asked Christ to enter my life: I said in my prayer, 'Lord, I don't know where this is going to take me, but I'm willing to go with you'.

As I look back on that turning around – for me quite abrupt, for many others very gradual – I have a strong sense that it was God searching for me, choosing me, rather than my searching for him, choosing him.

Christians have broken each other's heads over this matter of whether God chooses, or we choose. No tidy, QED sort of answers will prove satisfactory:

There was a young man who said 'Damn!
At last I've found out what I am:
A creature that moves in determinate grooves –
In fact not a bus but a tram.'   (R. A. Knox)

St Paul took us all into deep water when he mused about God's chosen people and the mystery of their unbelief: there are three chapters of it in the Letter to the Romans (9–11). Who is chosen and who is not remains a mystery. Yet the key word, appearing nine times in those difficult chapters, is mercy, the mercy of God to all people. Amazingly God is saying 'those who were not my people, I will call my people, and the unloved nation I will call my beloved' (Rom. 9:25). It is a very special experience for those who have felt shut out from the life of God's people to find themselves called 'my people'.

So if we have that conviction that by his mercy we have been chosen, what next? What have we been chosen for? There are some terrible examples of what follows from a Church or a nation saying, 'we are his chosen people'. The godly Puritans went to New England in the seventeenth century to find freedom to worship as they wanted. They met to discuss the Indian question. They passed the following resolutions:

1. The earth is the Lord's and the fullness thereof: Voted.
2. The Lord may give the earth, or any part of it to his chosen people: Voted.
3. We are his chosen people: Voted.

They were discussing the Indian question: their theology made it clear that Indians had no rights, so God's chosen people could take their land.

What have we been chosen for? The people of God in the Old Testament and New Testament know that they have been chosen, not for their own sake, but in order to serve God in the world. We are to be a servant Church, servant to God and servant in encountering others. We only begin to be what God wants us to be, as we start to be burden-bearers, taking on the stresses which others bear.

II. Archbishop Derek Worlock

I come of parents who were both converts to Roman Catholicism. My father went to Oxford with a view to ministry but interestingly thought better of it and became first a journalist and then a politician. My mother was a suffragette. I was the only Catholic boy at my prep school and my earliest ecumenical encounter was when another boy said that the pope was a rude word. In the spirit of apologetics of those days, we resorted to fisticuffs. The headmaster intervened, said that he would have no religious discrimination in his

school and took us both to his room for a beating. Sub-
sequently my adversary won a posthumous VC in Burma;
and I was made a bishop: not quite such a moving personal
conversion as that just related by Bishop Sheppard.

If my earliest experiences were unfortunate – I was some
years later ordered out of Lambeth by Archbishop Fisher for
what with some justification he called 'Roman aggression' –
it was probably because encounters of those days seldom
implied a meeting of minds, or any real communication at
all. One of you went under the steam-roller or you bounced
off. I think that I smarted most under the assumption that
as a Catholic of the Roman variety I must be either Italian
or more likely Irish. This was particularly frustrating during
the war, but even where there were good personal relationships there were fairly strict lines of demarcation. When as a
newly-ordained priest I had a baptism of fire in the worst of
London air raids, I had always to try to make sure that the
dead and the dying to whom I was called to minister was
'one of us'. It was not always clear on what one based that
assumption, even when the Civil Defence workers in the
rubble called out, 'Here, Padre, here's one of yours'.

This distinction within 'others' of 'one of ours – or theirs'
was a quite profound principle of separation, which sadly was
not always one of respect. When, some twenty-one years ago
now, Bishop Sheppard and I first met, before I went to work
in London's East End where he was already established, it
was more with a view to sharing interesting spiritual and
pastoral ideas than with very profound expectation of working
together in the service of others. It was at the time when the
Second Vatican Council was in progress: some days I had
the joyful contrast of sitting in a docker's flat at night after a
morning of high-powered theological expertise in the Vatican
that morning. But more important we were discovering the
nature of the Church, the relationship between Christians
who yet were divided in faith, and – marvel of marvels – the
bond of baptism into Christ's life and mission: that, once we
had come to accept the validity of each other's baptism.

That day of recognition of each other's baptism was probably the most important day in my life. It transformed our

relationship with one another, and gave new dimensions and direction to our work together in the service of others – now no longer just 'our own'.

Not that it all happened overnight. Those who in the past had doffed their hats to one another out of respect, but from across the street, now attended each other's Christmas Fairs. Perhaps because the practice of religion was such a personal thing, there was still the fear of 'poaching' – a more English and gentlemanly word than 'proselytising' – but it took another decade before we began to talk about partnership among Christians and acknowledged that help could be sought and given out of the bond of Christian love, without crossing the floor of God's house. Even then it was seldom more than Christians working alongside one another, which is not at all the same thing as working together.

Future historians will have a fascinating task trying to discern the issues which have drawn Christians into common mission. It is already said that it was the racial issues of the 1960s which brought Christians in the USA out on the streets together, arms linked, singing freedom songs and discovering the joy as well as the strength of being together with someone who believed in Jesus as the Son of God but perhaps worshipped in a very different way. In Liverpool it came to us before the Toxteth riots of 1981. It started with a single answer from the Churches to the government in response to its attempt to consult each Church severally about Inner Areas Studies. Soon after that I was approached under cover of darkness by representative shop stewards from a factory threatened with closure, who had been declined a meeting with the management in London. So together all of us marched side by side at the head of the protest demo through the streets of the city. The cameras clicked, the microphones appeared – and the management saw the men's representatives two days later. Attitudes changed that day. And so did the 'others' whom we encountered at the rallying point and who then marched behind us.

III. Bishop David Sheppard

When divided communities live their separate lives they feed on myths. Stories are told about the others, without anyone questioning their truth. Christians follow the man for others. If we know what it is to be chosen, to be accepted by Christ, to belong to his people, that should give us the security to reach out beyond our own group to the others, unpopular as that may be with our own group.

That means not letting people get away with it, when they are feeding on myth, or repeating slogans. During the miners' strike the Bishop of Sheffield told a small group of urban bishops to which I belong that he had recently visited a number of pits. A young man on the picket line had said, 'The working class have never got anything without fighting.' 'What do you mean?' the Bishop of Sheffield asked him.

We must not let other groups get away with myths either. When managers in the south-east of England say, 'New technology always produces new jobs', we too should say, 'What do you mean?' Does new technology always produce new jobs for everyone? Between the 1971 and 1981 censuses the number of managers even in Merseyside actually increased by some thousands. But the number of jobs for manual workers, skilled, semi-skilled and unskilled, altogether collapsed. Unemployment does not fall evenly on all groups. It falls on predictable areas and it falls on predictable groups.

So if comfortable Britain, successful Britain, wants to reach out to the other Britain, the hurt Britain, how can they do it? How can you help if you want to?

A lot starts from attitude. Many professional and middle-class families talk about 'these people' and blame them for not succeeding in life according to the yardsticks by which comfortable Britain measures success. If you ever catch yourself talking about 'these people', whoever they are, remember that text of mine: 'those who were not my people, I will call my people' (Rom. 9:25). That goes for you, and it goes for them. 'These people' are known by God as 'my people'.

I have been serving on the Archbishop of Canterbury's Commission on Urban Priority Areas. One of the subjects we have debated long and hard is about how commuter Christians and parishes can help bring about change for those who live in urban priority areas. Commuters have more influence than they suppose on the opportunities which inner city people have. The commuters are often the gatekeepers of opportunity, opening doors or shutting them on jobs, promotion, mortgages, bank loans, hire purchase, standards of health care, schools, transport and much more. One black woman told me of visiting a major firm in the London area on behalf of the Commission for Racial Equality. The managing director said to her, 'You won't find any prejudice here. We have many black people working in the factory.' She said, 'How do you get to be like you?' He said, 'You probably begin as an apprentice and work your way up.' 'Tell me about last year's apprentices,' she said, 'how many were there?' 'Eighty.' 'How many were female?' 'Four.' 'How many were black?' 'Zero.' If he is serious about the claim that there is no prejudice, he must monitor all applications for jobs and all promotion decisions. And he must send for them once a month. Then people will know that he means business.

Commuter Christians can help those at a disadvantage whom God calls 'my people' by greater involvement in whatever political party they choose. Many people in commuter land vote their fears. It is part of the responsibility of Christians to question fears and myths about 'these people'. They could involve themselves in a project through offering money or their skills or their time. If so, it must be done with respect for 'my people' and not trying to control them.

And for you? Perhaps that change of attitude from 'these people' to 'my people' may call you to go and live in urban priority areas, or in the third world, or to take your skills there. Perhaps it will bring a new set of priorities to the decision-making in industry or Civil Service or government in which you may be involved. Perhaps it will take you into one of the 'caring professions' or a different part of the teaching or medical professions. Perhaps the God whom you are meeting through your encounter with others will call you to serve as a priest or minister or deaconess. If that is his calling to you, it will stretch you to the limit and give you the most fulfilling life I know.

When you encounter people, be it your own grouping or 'the others', keep your eyes open, because if you have eyes to see, to notice, you may encounter the living God. It might be when you see the steady courage of one who will not let his own group get away with myths and slogans. It might be when you see an inner city mother refusing to give up against impossible odds, or a teacher keeping his expectations high of what children in a priority area can achieve against many disappointments.

Of course you may have to change your yardsticks for success, but if you encounter God I think you would have to do that anyway.

IV. Archbishop Derek Worlock

Encounters are not just ships passing in the night or even some sort of collision or bouncing-off. A true encounter is the sort of meeting when those encountering one another actually affect one another, when there is a rubbing off which makes a difference – for better or for worse. To be realistic, some encounters enhance a relationship, some provide a set-back. Some are very easy because there is a sharing of interests, an ease of relationship because of a natural affinity. But it is not always so. If as Christians we are really trying to encounter and recognise Christ in our neighbour, we have to face up to the fact that Christ, hungering for our concern, is present in the most abject and sometimes, humanly speaking, in the least attractive form. Perhaps that is where those who relate to one another more easily have to stand by with what we nowadays call 'mutual support'.

As leaders of Churches, seeking to serve the needs of the community, Bishop Sheppard and I have often to go together into the den of the lion – or even occasionally the lioness. Our approach to a problem is not always identical – at least in method – and sometimes on the doorstep I may say to him, 'Have you got your shining armour with you today?'

Perhaps there may be some chance to pray together for guidance and the right balance of silvery-tongued wisdom with principled firmness. But we receive great support in prayer from those for whom we try to speak. I shall never forget how early one morning we shivered in the reception area of the massive offices of some king of industry to whom we were going to deliver a final plea for a work-force about to be made redundant. We received the summons to go up in the lift and as we moved forward the girl in the reception desk stopped us and said, 'I too am a Christian, and I'd like you to know that while you are up there doing your thing, I'll be praying for you.'

Each day we encounter God in others, but his voice and his message are not always what you may anticipate, nor indeed is the person who is his mouthpiece always as conscious of Christian faith as that girl in the reception desk. This is where the two aspects of the encounter are important. It is one thing to be able to listen and recognise the message of Christ in those you encounter. It is another to be conscious that Christ's message and way must be evident in you to those you encounter. In many ways the latter is more difficult but it raises the whole question of how, by your bearing, by your manner of approach, by the service you give, you are able to affirm faith in good people who do not regard themselves as having faith, people whose views will be described by the pundits as a kind of folk-religion, whose religious practice is at best spasmodic, but in whom Christ dwells to be encountered if only we can get over our pre-conceived ideas about what he looks like.

And I want to close by giving two examples from South America where I have six Liverpool priests working. My joy is to visit and work with them. Two years ago I was in Peru, outside Chimbote where following terrible weather there had been an immense mud-slide from the Andes engulfing the shanty town I was visiting. One young Liverpool priest showed me a bamboo and clay lean-to which was his chapel and cheerfully said to me, 'It was great here at Christmas, actually offering midnight mass in conditions worse than those in which Jesus was born.' As I tried to come to terms with this we spotted a small boy sitting on a bench in the darkness. The priest asked him his name. 'Jesus,' was the reply. The priest smiled and asked him if he knew who the first Jesus was. The boy thought, pointed his finger at himself and said, 'Me.' Then he got up and shambled out, dragging a paralysed arm and leg. We found out later that this was the result of a dirty syringe used by a Relief Agency inoculating the area.

That same priest wrote to me recently. He is now high in the mountains south of Lima. I would like to share part of his letter:

People here are simple. Dates, days, time, mean nothing. This morning there was a wedding. They were only half an hour late. Feeling very positive, I had just got to the end of the wedding ceremony when a man walked up to me behind the altar with a paper in his hand, saying, 'Marry us as well, Padre.' I wanted to say, 'You can't just walk up here like this' . . . I limited myself to saying, 'Not now, see me after Mass.'

The couple were really victims of circumstances. What threw me was that they had planned to marry on 29 December in their own village. I had been due to go there for Mass that day. I got stuck in Andahuaylas with no petrol to be had anywhere. I had to send a message to cancel the trip. I knew nothing of the wedding anyway. The couple heard that the Padres did weddings on Mondays in Huancarama. They had walked the fifteen kilometres . . . it seemed perfectly reasonable for them to turn up on the off-chance and tag along. I went back to the church with them and started the wedding.

The bride had bare feet. She fed her baby off and on during the ceremony. Just the two of them with two *padrinos* or sponsors. The groom wore his sandals made of tyres; his trousers were patched on both knees; a filthy shirt and pullover full of holes. So they came the wrong day . . .

I thought of Mary and Joseph. They were simple peasants too. I bet they turned up in Bethlehem on the wrong day; brought the wrong documents and joined the wrong queue. I shouldn't be surprised if they were told to come back tomorrow or even next week a few times by Roman officials.

May we all encounter Christ in others all our days and have the humble faith to recognise him.

7

Exploring the depths: why pray?

PETER BALL, Founder of the Community of the Glorious Ascension and for seventeen years its Prior, and now Bishop of Lewes, writes on the 'extraordinary activity' we call prayer.

I want to try to say three things about why we pray and in outline they are these. First of all – and I use the word 'I' because I don't want to pressurise in any way – I have prayed because I cannot help it; it is written into my creation. That is first. Secondly I have prayed because of the incarnation, because of the fascination of God, especially in Christ. And thirdly I have prayed because it has brought sparkle and dark meaning and redemptive power to life.

Prayer, surely, is the strangest activity of man, possibly communicating with nothing, which will nevertheless not go away, however much the transcendent seems to be disproved, however much God is made irrelevant. Men and women of every possible mixture of intellect and nature still kneel or simply turn to address an invisible being who seems to leave so little evidence of his being, so few inescapable proofs of his presence. More than this, they adore, they purport to obey, they prostrate and reveal themselves to this uncreature. In Cambridge we can sit within a hundred yards of countless buildings which have been created at vast expense and are still being maintained at even greater expense, simply for this extraordinary activity of exploring the depths of worshipping an invisible God; and all this expense for such a performance still goes on in a starving world. For a detached observer, much of what we have done so far in this book is fairly easy to grasp. Man could invent a God in the same way as he can invent the detachment of number in mathematics and then enjoy the intellectual workout of 'why I believe' and 'what I believe' and even 'why I don't believe'. But crazily into these places of worship come otherwise rational human beings to sing and to talk, to perform extraordinary rituals of prayer and worship, to a perhaps physical emptiness, to a mysterious non-presence. It has been said that the only other activity even vaguely resembling this is, of course, cricket. Yet out of this activity has come so much that is the height of man's achievements. The silence of the wilderness of Goshen trembles into a burning bush of prayer which leads Moses on an astounding journey of rescue from which the western world will never recover. Sixteen years by himself in a cave in central Italy, communing, agonising, caught up in ecstasy with this presence, prepared the young Benedict in the fifth century to found that group of prayer-men and women from whom has sprung most of what we value in our life today – education, medicine, art, music, architecture. In modern times if we were to wonder what was the foundation of the glorious rescue work of Mother Teresa, as countless young women, capable of so much else, search the dustbins of Calcutta for dying and deprived children, what went before was twenty years of Mother Teresa in a conventional prayer life in one of those awesome pre-Vatican II convents.

It is almost impossible to suppose that these saints and countless others have not met someone in that prayer and worship, someone who has imparted inspiration and vision about sublime things for the enriching of life, a transfiguration which in art and music becomes tangible beauty and goodness. Yet more mysteriously still, like a Gothic arch they point beyond themselves, perhaps even to the source of that inspiration. It seems harder, for me anyway, to see these wonders coming out of the auto-suggestion of the saints and worshippers, than from a meeting with a divine person. To say that prayer is a way of pulling the handle of the fruit-machine and, after much whirling of the numbers, a fresh jackpot of Chartres Cathedral emerges, strains my credulity even more than the idea of meeting someone in prayer. As

Dr Eamon Duffy has said, the faces of those who have been exposed to this prayer object for years and years shine with a light which is so unmistakably beautiful that we are compelled to ask, not so much, 'What have you been doing for twenty years?' but 'Who have you been with all this time, for he's so beautiful?' So I prayed because, like so many others, I must.

And here may I make a slight detour, because this chapter is called 'Exploring the Depths' when I think I have been talking about the heights. I find the title difficult, for it smacks of that spirituality of the sixties and the seventies when we were all exploring the ground of our being. We were all on a journey inwards with all the individualistic undertones of 'coming to the fullness of my being', 'becoming what I really am'. I suppose there must be some truth there, for some have found gold rather than just knobbly artichokes in the ground of their being, but I find it rather narcissistic. Certainly to be able to forgive myself for being such a failure, so unkind, so repugnant to my hopes of myself, is so awful an inward task that to be able to meet God embracing my inward self-unforgivingness is wonderful.

But this overall approach to spirituality seems to me to lack space, to be claustrophobic without the freedom of Mozart and the openness of Bach. It is rather like my experience as a child. Like most five-year-olds, I suppose, I used to play houses down my bed at night, disappearing inwards and downwards, rather like that kind of prayer, into different parts of my bed which I had designated as the dining room and the drawing room and the larder. Sadly it all ended rather dramatically when I tried to do some real cooking in the space allotted for the kitchen. And I think that is rather the end of that kind of prayer. Strangely too, the best contemplatives have never been the inward lookers. The Carthusians, the severest of all the enclosed orders, tell me that the best monks come from extrovert rugby-playing doctors – very good contemplatives. There, then, is the strangest of all human activity, I believe. And in its strangeness we meet God and out of it has come this extraordinary fullness of life.

67

Now, if we really do meet God in prayer, it may be important just for a moment to look at this God whom we meet. What is he like? What sort of person is making relationships with us? As Rahner said, to look at the face of the crucified is to know that we shall be spared nothing. To face God in prayer is to be invited into the whole of his transfiguring, loving and redeeming activity. How else could our Lord treat his friends than by sharing all of himself with them? It is the mark of all true friendship.

I want to try to show you in language that Jesus himself used, what he shared of himself with his disciples and what he shares with us in prayer. With the light but trusting touch of Mozart, I want to try to see how in his parables Jesus actually takes us to the boundaries of where religion can and does shut out life, of where morality does and can encase love, of where hypocrisy stifles true faith and of where establishment binds us to wrong loyalties. And in the end we shall see that because Jesus goes over those boundaries he is broken and in the breaking of his life he gives life. But I think it may be easy in the lightness to miss the depths.

Jesus looked at his congregation and he said to them, as he leaned towards them, 'The kingdom of heaven is like chips, which a woman dropped into deep, hot fat until they were brown all over.' And they looked at him as if he was mad. 'Yes,' he said. 'It's like chips or like a runner bean, the smallest of all beans, which a man took and he pushed it down with his heel in the ground and it sprang up and he put sticks in it and he sat in his kitchen and saw the birds among the big green leaves. Love,' he said, 'is so overflowing, it overflows all our ideas. It's like a farmer out at Madingley who to avoid death duties divided his great big farm between his two sons. And James found a most delicious popsy in the Blue Boar and off they went to the South of France and they had a whale of a time. And the money ran out and he telephoned from Liverpool Street and Dad said, "Is that you James? Gosh, your Mum and I have been longing to see you. We'll meet you at Cambridge Station." ' And they looked at Jesus and they said, 'If that's the sort of morality he's preaching, then the sooner he's out of the way, the better.'

Jesus said, 'You know, love can only be destroyed by hypocrites and pride. In fact it was', he said, 'totally destroyed by a woman living in Grange Road who had a supper party. She started flirting with somebody else's husband and at first, of course, it was quite innocent, then it became a serious affair. Then she had a flaming row with her husband who forgave her all. And the next day she was walking down King's Parade and she saw a woman whom she thought had said something unpleasant about her and she cut her dead.' Jesus said, 'That woman will pay for every moment of her flirtation in the pains of hell.' And Jesus saw as he looked that sadly most people that he was speaking to had not even the courage to flirt and he began to play with them. He said, 'You've all got darning needles, haven't you? Big eyes in darning needles,' he said. 'Great big eyes. Have you ever tried to get an elephant through them? Oh yes,' he said, 'start with the tail, it's easier that way. Oh yes, get your foot behind.' And they began to enjoy this a lot. 'Oh yes, but you realise that if any of us have riches,' said he, 'that's our chance of getting into the kingdom of God. That's our chance.'

Jesus saw that the anger was beginning to rise and he told them one last story about a lovely Englishman, humble and kind, who had nevertheless done rather well in the city. He filled his beautiful house with rejected young people, whom he and his wife cared for and loved with that free and strange concern that quiet men and women can give, and he was determined that they should also serve their country and the world well and cleanly, but with a choice that was theirs. One went into the Civil Service, one as an executive into a large union, another into an advertising company. Their goodness and their honesty, despite their humility, slowly became a threat to their employers and the Civil Servant was accused of dishonesty, easily arranged in high quarters; he was sentenced and imprisoned. The union man was accused of disloyalty to the party and was ignominiously sacked. Ah, but he had a son of his own, the joy of his life, his only child;

he could serve our Queen and country in the Royal Air Force in this time of crisis. 'How was it then,' said Jesus, 'that after three years of increasing fear of his beautiful openness, the father received a telephone call one evening from an impeccable RAF man saying that his son had died slowly and painfully in an unexplained fire while taking off? "Just an accident, sir", said the officer. "There will be a full enquiry of course." ' The anger rose in Jesus's hearers and their anger turned to hatred and their hatred to violence and God's elect establishment took the man of love, the man of parables, and they found, as you know, wood and nails and they hammered out their fears and hatred into soft hands and soft feet and they nailed him out like an animal's skin, stretched for curing in the hot sun.

And that was that. But I have often wondered whether, as they lay on their silk beds, they just heard the creak or the moan of a great stone moving, the odd snatch of an angel's hymn. For not even death could hold this man of love, this man of parables, and I believe he is standing among us tonight. Of course my constant prayer is that the mess he got himself into two thousand years ago will avail for my mess. And I say these parables, not to cajole us, but to illustrate the fascination that Christ has, the extraordinary way in which prayer draws people to meet this man of the gospel. That is the point; that in prayer countless men and women have found that he not only cleans their filth, as once he knelt and washed some dirty apostolic feet, but he allows us to share his person and his redeeming work, both in its joys and in its costs; and here are those depths which are not mine, but his. One thing alone he asked, and strangely that is the most unromantic of all the virtues, and that is perseverance, the battle to go on going on. That is all our Lord talks about, about prayer, takes us into all those conflicts of continual tiredness, of the continual effort of concentration, of the continual choice of loyalties, which all sound muscular rather than mystical and which are of a naked will rather than a heavenly embrace. These are the areas, of course, where all the great battles of men, not only of prayer, are fought either alone or corporately and where the spoils of victory are rich.

So if we hold fast, exploring the depths, we will realise and share with Christ the joy and struggle of man's journey back from sin. In today's world there is that extraordinary pain which is involved in the divine mopping-up operation where the victory has been won, but where the snipers are still many.

I want to say just a few more things about this sharing. It will be an experience filled with the silence of love. It will mean a strange living on the boundaries of convention such as I pointed to in those parables of Jesus. It will mean going back to the simplicity of the wilderness, not because the world is evil in itself, but because the intense embrace of the lover must be naked. It is to come to the heart to which all else is straining and longing, which is why the Eucharist must be the central friendship; in that place we do not come principally for edification, or even for means of grace for our daily lives, nor for some take-away spirituality centred in ourselves. There in the Eucharist we become who we really are as Christians: the Word incarnate, the high priests of creation bringing in life to God; and then finally the Holy Communion as the consummation of lovers, the bond of fellowship, the bread of life and the blood of redemption to the world. We truly share his life ready to be worked out elsewhere.

It is wonderfully said, as you know, by George Herbert in 'The Agonie':

> Philosophers have measur'd mountains,
> Fathom'd the depths of seas, of states, and kings,
> Walk'd with a staffe to heav'n, and traced fountains:
>   But there are two vast, spacious things,
> The which to measure it doth more behove:
> Yet few there are that sound them; Sinne and Love.

> Who would know Sinne, let him repair
> Unto Mount Olivet; there shall he see
> A man so wrung with pains, that all his hair,
>   His skinne, his garments bloudie be.
> Sinne is that presse and vice, which forceth pain
> To hunt his cruell food through ev'ry vein.

71

Who knows not Love, let him assay
And taste that juice, which on the crosse a pike
Did set again abroach; then let him say
    If ever he did taste the like.
Love is that liquor sweet and most divine,
Which my God feels as bloud; but I, as wine.

And so to the final part. I have prayed because for me it brings sparkle and even dark meaning and redemptive power into life. As I have said, we do not pray principally for help, for comfort, for request, for edification, but because prayer and worship are the centre of the whole story. In prayer we come home. We become real. We become our great vocation to be the mouthpiece of creation praising God. We are drawn into the company of Christ with his angels and saints where wholeness belongs and it is from this centre, and of course in it, that everything else comes to life. People become entirely different when we see them through prayer, not sentimentally glamorous, but gorgeous, because they are seen with the eyes of God. I can then even put up with that awful brother monk sniffing next to me in chapel every day if I see him through the eyes of God – just! It is because of his or her prayer that people crowd to a holy man or woman for advice, even if he has been shut up in a monastery for years, because he sees clearly both bad and good, for he sees from the centre. Then again, prayer is what makes us dance down the street at the joy of living, as young lovers dance through the fields in the old cigarette advertisements on the television. Prayer also makes us weep in agony over Ethiopia. Prayer takes away the restraints of status and achievement, bringing the freedom which reveals truth. It brings life to living, even to nature and the arts. I often have people come and sit on the sofa in my room and look out through the window with the marvellous view of the Sussex Downs, and some of them suddenly turn away and say, 'Oh, I must thank God'; and I say, 'Come off it, man, enjoy it in God; stop the thanking business, you can enjoy it in God.' And in the arts I think of Karl Barth's famous saying that when the angels play for the glory of God they play Bach, when they play for their own amusement they play Mozart. This is all very hard to express, but prayer is the secret spring of life in which is the atmosphere of that nudging relationship with God which is sheer wonder at being with him and which gives colour to living. Again George Herbert:

> This is the famous stone
>   That turneth all to gold:
> For that which God doth touch and own
>   Cannot for lesse be told.
>
> (from 'The Church')

Finally and strangely, not only does prayer do this to the world, it is the light which lightens religion. We can shield behind religion. We can turn on our religiosity that numbs us to reality. The other day a priest died and we had just screwed him down in his coffin and brought him into church and the whole church stood within two feet of him, the choir in their red funny hats, and what did we sing, looking at the coffin, without realising it, but 'Stand up, stand up for Jesus'. I said to the archdeacon, 'Do you hear what they are singing?' He said, 'Yes,' without realising. I said, 'What do you think the chances are?' Nobody had seen it. My brother went to a service for diabetics where they sang, 'How sweet the name of Jesus sounds'. We get numb to religion. Prayer will deal with this. Prayer will bring reality to that simplistic unreality which is so common nowadays in our services. If the Victorians were known for their sentimentality I think we shall be known for our triteness, typified by some choruses which are based on 'Jesus, I love you (three times)'. Prayer will bring life and reality to all this, but above all it reveals the truth in the gospel word and in the Holy Communion as the consummation of lovers, as I have said. Even the grinding prayer has strength in the darkness because of the prayer that is gone before.

So there it is. Prayer is the sparkle, even the dark meaning behind life. In speaking of it I have named the only thing that a Christian cannot do without. There are times when he or she may be separated from word, sacrament, and even fellowship. Prayer remains.

8

Can you be a Christian and not go to church?
Does God punish us?

Those who dismiss Christianity are often dismissing a hotch-potch of received ideas which are a travesty of what informed Christians believe. Each day of the Encounters week, at lunchtime in the Roman Catholic chaplaincy, speakers dealt with popular misconceptions. Two scintillating addresses by Dr Rowan Williams on the humanity and divinity of Jesus were delivered from the briefest of notes; sadly, pressure of work has prevented him from preparing a full manuscript for this book.

In this chapter UNA KROLL, an Anglican deaconess who formerly worked as a doctor in London and Africa, tackles two questions.

I. Can you be a Christian and not go to church?

Your own answer to this loaded question will be influenced by your understanding of what is involved in becoming a Christian and belonging to a Church whose members meet for worship in a church. The answer may therefore differ according to your cultural background, upbringing, present opinion, temperament and habitual religious custom. I stress this at the outset because I hope to show that there are different ways of approaching this question and several satisfying answers to it, providing that we can tolerate each other's differences and particular needs.

Some people find it relatively simple to see a close connection between being a Christian and going to church. They are born into and grow up within a local denominational community of Christians who meet in a building called a church which has been set aside for worship. They never question the doctrines, tenets or practices of their faith. Their beliefs are strong and individual, shaped partly by what they have been taught from early childhood and partly by experiences which may affirm or contradict what they have learnt. At the opposite extreme there are those who either have no experience of life in a Christian family or have been disillusioned by their own experience of institutional church life. They equate going to church with being a Christian and if they do not like what goes on in church or what they know of Christians they reject Christianity as well. When they turn away from going to church they also become indifferent or hostile to Christianity. In doing that they have declared their own belief in the connection between faith and church-going. Both groups of people have made choices which are settled and do not require further examination or anxiety.

To these two groups of people who accept as natural and inevitable the logic of the link between being a Christian and going to a church I would add a third group, namely those who have been converted to Christian discipleship by a personal encounter with Christ and who thereafter find themselves at home in a Christian community which satisfies their every need. St Paul springs to mind as someone who moved from a position of antagonism towards Christians he had heard about, met and persecuted, to one of dedicated discipleship to the person whom he met on the road to Damascus. In his subsequent teachings and witness Paul stresses the need for Christians to come together for worship, mutual upbuilding and service as together they seek to witness to the fact that they are called to be the body of Christ, his agents in the world.

Later Christian history is studded with many examples of men and women who were converted by similar personal encounters and became great leaders in their own times and examples for us today. When I was a young woman I remember, for instance, being greatly moved by hearing about an agnostic doctor with an enquiring mind who found himself challenged to read the gospels. As he did so he became aware of a presence so compelling, so attractive, so recognisable as the person he was reading about in the Bible, that he knew instantly that his life would be totally changed by that encounter with the living person of Christ made present in his life, at that moment, in that room, within himself. He surrendered his life, his ambitions, himself, and later became an Orthodox monk, a priest and a bishop. People like this man, Anthony Bloom, whose lives have been touched by God in this way do not forget that kind of moment. Their conviction about its reality and importance in shaping their lives seems to carry them into the Church and helps them to live creative Christian lives in and through the formative discipline of going to church to worship God and be with other Christians so that together they can serve the world in which they live.

The conversions and lives of such men and women of God can serve to encourage those of us who have never known a comparable experience in our own lives but who can accept its validity in other people's lives. So one answer to the question, 'Can you be a Christian and not to go to church?' is, 'Possibly, but the link is so close that it's natural for Christians to want to go to church, so why stay away?' And it is important to note that millions of people are able to identify Christ with his Church. Equally, though, millions of people are so dissatisfied with the Church, as they find it in their local churches, that they reject Christ along with the Christian community that seems such a sinful and human institution in their own neighbourhood. So perhaps even those of us who are quite happy about going along to our local church should ask ourselves again whether it is possible to be a Christian and yet not go to church?

Now, many people do feel it is quite possible to be a committed Christian, live according to the gospel teachings of Christ, yet never belong to the Church as a church-going Christian. Some who say such things do so because it is a kind of excuse for not getting out of bed on a Sunday morning. Some say they can remain Christians only because they do not go to church and they imply that the local Christians are more awful and far less loving than many other people who do not call themselves Christian, so by staying away they feel closer to God and Christ than if they go to church with people whom they see as 'hypocrites' or 'luke-warm' or 'lip-service' Christians. Some drop out from going along to church because they 'get nothing out of the service' or 'have nothing in common with the people who are there'. It will not do for those of us who do continue to go to church, who are 'paid up' Christians, by which I mean Christians who are content to be identified with the tenets and customs of a particular local church within a particular branch of a denominational Church, to criticise people whom we have failed in some way. Instead we need to ask ourselves what we mean exactly by 'Church' and 'going to church'. Here I need to digress for a few moments to consider the lives of two well known people, Dag Hammarskjold and Simone Weil, who understood more about Christianity than most of us do, who followed Christ more closely than most of us ever will, and who yet remained outside the church-going Christian community. If we do this I believe we shall come to understand 'going to church' in a different way.

Dag Hammarskjold (1905–61) lost his faith at university. Then, over a long peroid as a businessman, government official and Secretary-General of the United Nations, he gradually journeyed back to faith until, towards the end of his life, on Whit Sunday 1961, he wrote in his diary:

I don't know Who – or what – put the question, I don't know when it was put. I don't even remember answering. But at some moment I did answer 'yes' to Someone – or Something – and from that hour I was certain that existence is meaningful and that, therefore, my life, in self-surrender, had a goal. From that moment I have known what it means 'not to look back', and 'to take no thought for the morrow'.[1]

Hammarskjold spent his life trying to bring peace to the world. On his last peace-seeking flight to the Congo, when his plane crashed and he was killed, he had with him, as always, a pocket edition of Thomas à Kempis's *Imitation of Christ*. He believed; he followed Christ; yet he never joined in the corporate, liturgical or sacramental life of any Church.

Simone Weil (1909–43), who was a distinguished Jewish

philosopher with an open mind and a thirst for knowledge, came to the Benedictine Abbey of Solesmes in 1938 as a guest. While she was there she had an intense mystical experience which she later wrote about to a friend: 'Christ came down and seized me,' she said.[2] Later she made friends with Fr Henri Perrin and became passionately interested in Catholic Christianity, though she refused to be baptised. In her own journey she came to believe that she was called to 'lay down her life for her friends', and to show her solidarity with French people, who were then living under German occupation, she refused to eat despite a serious illness. She died of starvation and pulmonary tuberculosis on 24 August 1943.

Here were two people who believed, who had personal encounters with Christ, very similar to those described by St Paul and Archbishop Anthony Bloom, and who remained 'outside the fold'. Why? We do not know exactly why they made the decisions they did. We for our part might not make the same decisions, yet we must surely feel that they partook of the baptism of believers who follow Christ. They were exceptional people, yet there is a sense in which I believe they represent a great many others who experience the Body of Christ in a mystical way, as an experiential reality, without belonging to the 'Church militant here on earth'.

I tread on dangerous ground. Yet, for me that ground is holy, and impels me to discard my shoes in order to worship God. You see it is belonging to that kind of Church that I really understand better than any other kind. It is in and through my union with Christ, in and through his graciousness in allowing me to belong to his Body, through the indwelling presence of the Holy Spirit, that I come to experience the Church of God. That Church has little to do with denominationalism or locality, yet it enables me to belong to my local Christian community with thankfulness. In going to church with other Christians, many of them very different people from myself, many of them people I would never ordinarily meet, I find hope and strength. I am glad that I am accepted, despite my faults and weaknesses. I am glad I can worship and work with people who hold different beliefs and opinions from myself, and who can help me to look at some of my own prejudices even while I am trying to help them to see their own. I am even glad that I can suffer a little at the hands of those who deride the Church and condemn us all as 'weaklings' and 'hypocrites'.

I go to church because I belong to the Church, yet in the Church I meet many people whom I do not meet in church. You could say that I have the best of both worlds, that I am hedging my bets, that I am not honouring Christ if I say that you can be a Christian without going to church. I would reply: 'Christians are the Church: they find each other in him, in church or out of it.' Yet, I would also add that, unlike Hammarskjold and Weil, I need to go to church and am happy to belong to my own local Christian community.

II. Does God punish us?

Any medical doctor like myself, who has spent over thirty years caring for patients, will have met a number of people who greet unexpected, serious, life–threatening illness, disaster or sudden bereavement with agonised questions: 'Why me?' 'Why should this terrible suffering come to my innocent child?' 'What have I done to deserve this?' 'Why is God punishing me?' These questions and feelings are real and poignant. Many people do feel that God does punish them and in their agony they recall all kinds of sins and misdemeanours that deserve such punishment. Which of us, after all, does not have something of which we need to repent?

When people are brave enough, honest enough and trusting enough to tell me about these deep feelings I do not feel inclined to fob them off with platitudes or truisms. I sense that they are reacting to their suffering with complex emotions which include anger and guilt: anger, because in most people's eyes a loving God would not punish in that way; guilt, because, maybe, if they had not committed that sin, of which they have suddenly become so aware, they would not be suffering at all. Alongside these emotions, yet often more hidden, comes fear, the kind of feeling that tells men and women that God, being Almighty, can be appeased, can forgive, can avert disaster, can heal even when the suffering is deserved. Anger with God is then seen by them as an emotion which can be dangerous and so it is often suppressed or even repressed. Instead attitudes of repentance, bargaining and petition are substituted. Nevertheless, healthy anger with an apparently punitive God can and does erupt on occasion, although it always seems easier to be angry with God on someone else's behalf rather than for oneself.

Clergy and doctors faced with such anguished questions often fall silent because they do not know what to say. Sometimes they try to defend God by asserting that a loving God always desires healing, not retribution. Often they try to reassure their clients that disease has natural causes which have nothing to do with a person's sin or faults. Nearly always they will try to help patients and clients who are suffering from such conflicting emotions by assuring them that Christ is with them in the suffering and will give them the strength to bear it. I have once or twice been on the receiving end of such help and I have to say that I did not find that anything assuaged my pain until I was given permission, and encouraged, to vent my anger on God who seemed to me, rightly or wrongly, to have been the author of my misfortune.

The idea that God punishes people is very common and when we ourselves are not the victims of this kind of treatment we are rather inclined to want God to punish those whom we judge to be evil-doers. Indeed, we can get some satisfaction out of seeing them get their just deserts. The Old Testament writers often implore God to defend them against their enemies and rejoice when their entreaties appear to be answered. Many of the psalms which the Christian churches use in their liturgical worship contain such sentiments. We want to see God acting justly, punishing those who need correction and honouring those who honour him. There have been some twentieth-century Christian writers who have supposed that such notions of retributive justice are too reminiscent of primitive ideas to hold much credibility in a modern scientific age. Primitive they may be, but they are still active in present-day society as can be seen when they surface from time to time as they have done in comparatively recent times. The idea that a loving God could punish a Church which appointed a supposedly unorthodox theologian as a diocesan bishop by burning up the beautiful cathedral in which he had been consecrated did not seem at all incongruous to those sincere Christians who saw God's justice in a flash of lightning. Some people might be able to laugh such thoughts off, but all of us must surely take seriously the notion that a future nuclear explosion might find favour with God as a precursor to Armageddon, the end of the world and the second coming of Christ. These ideas are voiced by many Christians: their danger lies in the fact that expectation enhances the likelihood of someone in power feeling that they will be doing God's will by becoming his agent of punishment.

It is therefore important that we address ourselves to this important question, 'Does God punish us?' sympathetically and attentively. I do not myself find it an easy question to answer. At the risk of over-simplification I want to say that I think there is a difference between *retribution* and *correction* in that, to my mind, God does not punish us retributively, although human beings wish that he would, and sometimes do that to each other. God can and does chastise those whom he loves. Let me illustrate what I am trying to say by the example of a mother who sees her child playing with matches. If she tells the child not to play with matches and the child responds by lighting one, which then burns its fingers, the fault is the child's, not the mother's; or so many people would say. The mother loves the child and comforts her when she is hurt, but the punishment itself is only the logical outcome of the child's disobedience. The punishment could be retributive if the mother did not warn the child that matches burn in order to ensure that the child suffered hurt, which somehow satisfied the mother's desire to see her own child in pain. Even if warning were given it is possible to find mothers who seem to enjoy seeing their children suffer. On the other hand, a loving mother might decide to warn the child what might happen if the child went on playing with the matches, yet deliberately not intervene at once when the child was disobedient so that the child could learn by experience that fire can hurt. Any loving mother would, of course, intervene before the child had hurt itself badly or set the house on fire. That kind of punishment, for the child's own good, might be considered to be a way of chastising the child out of motives of love. A slap on the hand or bottom might effect the same kind of end result in that the child might learn to be good by suffering a lesser evil than the one that might accrue to her through natural causes. There are those of us who would say that no loving mother could stand by and permit her child to suffer if she could help it, but that if her child was unavoidably hurt, despite all the mother's admonitions and loving care, then the mother would suffer as well as the child.

My description of a human situation which occurs in most families at one time or another, if not in relation to matches, then certainly in relation to other incidents in family life, gives us some clues about God's relation towards us in regard to the punishment or chastisement of sin. Sin sometimes reaps its own reward. Our sufferings, punishments and hurts are often self-inflicted, individually or collectively. We cannot hold God responsible for that. God is a just God and justice acts indifferently so that sometimes punishment is inevitable, yet God's punishment is not retributive in the way that human beings sometimes inflict punishment on each other, as a sadistic mother might do if she were to take pleasure in seeing her child burnt. God is no sadist, yet there is a sense in which his justice makes our punishment inevitable at times. God loves us enough to chastise us on occasion, not in a vengeful way, but in a way that helps us to correct our mistakes and to learn from them.

This discussion would be incomplete if we ended without thinking about the way in which God allowed his own Son to endure punishment at the hands of human beings. When God ordained that punishment was a form of justice he also made a way of escape when he permitted his own Son to suffer death in order that we might be redeemed from the ultimate consequences of our sins. In that work of atonement Christ's role and sufferings are unique. It is as if the mother rushed forward to save the child and took upon herself the hurt that the child deserved; yet even that analogy does not compass the mystery of the atonement.

If, then, I am asked whether I believe that God punishes us, I have to answer affirmatively because I believe in God's justice, and yet I also believe in God's mercy and trust in his love. I can therefore never think of God as one who delights in retribution, but I can accept his chastisement and share its burden as a member of Christ's body, the Church, knowing that the suffering that I experience as a punishment comes from the hand of a loving God who wills only our ultimate good. I am not afraid to feel angry with God on occasion and I whimper like anyone else when I am hurt and frightened. Somehow I also know that Christ who knew the full weight of suffering in his human life, and who endures it until his work will be completed through his second coming, suffers whenever we suffer justly or innocently, as a mother does when her child is hurt, and that gives me courage and comfort because I know that I am not alone. Such love towards me and all mankind inspires me to hope that a time will come when there will be an end to death and to mourning and crying and pain, for the old order will have passed away. There are times when I catch a glimpse of the New Jerusalem even now.

Notes

1. Dag Hammarskjold, *Markings*. 1964.
2. Lawrence S. Cunningham, in *Dictionary of Christian Spirituality*. 1983.

9

What does it mean to believe that the Bible is true?

Father TIMOTHY RADCLIFFE is Prior of Blackfriars, Oxford, and a former Roman Catholic Chaplain to the University of London. In Chapters 9 and 10 he tackles two questions on belief.

What would it mean to say that I believed that the whole of the Bible was true? It implies that I am committed to believing an indefinite number of things. I might have thought that I had managed to believe everything in the Bible; but what if someone were then to produce some new and indigestible item for faith, like Jonah being swallowed by a whale, or Balaam's conversation with his donkey? So how could I ever know that I believed everything in the Bible to be true?

I think that this is a false quandary which only arises if we let ourselves be trapped into imagining that belief in the truth of the Bible demands assent to a large number of discrete and separate facts, from the existence of Adam and Eve, through the call of Abraham and the Exodus, to the resurrection of Christ and the second coming. But as Christians we are committed to believing only one thing; that of being saved by the life, death and resurrection of Christ. We believe the rest of the Bible to be true not in addition to that event, but as telling us what sort of an event it was. Let us imagine that someone said that they believed in the New Testament but could not accept the Old Testament. It sounds as if they are believing fewer things than someone who accepts the whole canon. They believe in Jesus but not in Abraham. But that would not be the essential difference. They would believe in Jesus differently. They would not see him as the final vindication of God's faithfulness to his people, the culmination of a long history of salvation. It would be a diminished faith not because of what it omitted about Abraham or Moses, but because of what it failed to say about Jesus. And if someone were to claim that they believed in the resurrection but not in Pentecost or the Church, then they would mean something different by the resurrection. It would be merely the escape from death by a single individual and not the birth of a new community. I do not believe in the story of Adam and Eve as giving me special information about the origins of humanity. That was not its purpose. The story of the Fall helps me to understand the predicament of mankind apart from God, and so what it means to be saved in Christ.

This may look like a weak interpretation of what it means to say that the Bible is true, an escape route from having to assent to all sorts of implausible claims. But it all depends upon what may be counted as a true description of an event. There is a common myth that the most objective description is one that simply tells you what happened without interpretation. The ideal witness is the uninvolved spectator, the dispassionate eye of the camera. And there are still a few people who think that to say that everything in the Bible is true is to claim that it gives that sort of an account. To believe in the story of Jonah and the whale is to claim that it describes what someone paddling by in a boat at the time would have seen. Fundamentalists have argued at length as to whether God created a special whale for the occasion or merely adapted an existing model. This looks like a way of taking the biblical text seriously, but this myth of the uninvolved spectator, the unprejudiced eye of the person who simply sees what is before him, is modern and western. It goes with a particular scientific tradition, a way of relating to the environment and an economic system. It would be highly subjective to try to impose that way of looking at the world on people who thought and lived quite differently. For them an objectively true account of an event would be one that showed how it belonged within the story of our lives. An increasing number of scholars now believe that the story of Abraham's call was written by exiles in Babylon in the sixth century BC. For them a true account of what happened would not tell us the exact date that he left for the Promised Land and plot his route on a map. It would explore how his call was a sign of hope for them. The story looks forward to the moment when his descendants would once again be brought to the Promised Land. That is a proper account of what happened to Abraham because it knits the event into the single story of God's dealings with his people. It has the objectivity of a story well told.

When we try to make sense of our own lives we are not taken in by this myth of the disinterested spectator. The most important moments can only be described by seeing how they echo the past and are filled with the promise of the future. We fall in love, make promises, fulfil ambitions, fail, make new beginnings, are born and die, all events that we understand by fitting them into the story of our lives as a whole. So then, to believe, as Christians, that the Bible is true is not to believe in innumerable discrete events, each of which requires a separate act of assent; it is to believe that they all, somehow, belong within the single story that reaches its climax in the death and resurrection of Christ. That is the measure of the meaning of the whole canon. Jesus said to the disciples on the road to Emmaus:

'O foolish men, and slow of heart to believe all that the prophets have spoken! Was it not necessary that the Christ should suffer these things and enter into his glory?' And beginning with Moses and all the prophets, he interpreted to them in all the scriptures the things concerning himself. (Luke 24:25–7)

This may help to explain why biblical writers can apparently contradict themselves when they are describing the same event. They explore what really happened by relating the event to the wider story in a variety of ways. Luke, for example, describes the Ascension twice, at the end of the gospel and at the beginning of Acts; and people are sometimes

troubled because the two accounts are historically incompatible. In the gospel it takes place on Easter day at Bethany,
and the disciples go to the temple to praise God; but in Acts
it happens forty days later on Mount Olivet, and the disciples
go back to the upper room. This is not because Luke is
absentminded or unconcerned with what *really* happened. He
tells us what *really* happened precisely by showing how the
Ascension is the linchpin of a story that started with Zech-
ariah in the temple and ends at the end of Acts with Paul
preaching in Rome. He shows us how it is an event that looks
both ways and so holds together the story of the life of Jesus
and that of the Church. It is the climax of Jesus's journey to
Jerusalem and the beginning of something new, the mission
of the Church to the ends of the earth. If Luke had really
been worried about contradicting himself on historical details
then he would never have given us three incompatible
accounts of Paul's conversion.

This raises further problems. It is all very well to say that
Luke is not attempting to give what we would count as a
historical account of the Ascension; he is exploring its
meaning. But unless something did in fact happen on Mount
Olivet, or Bethany, then there would have been no event to
have a rich meaning. The camera might not have been able
to catch the deep mystery of the Ascension; maybe that could
only be told through a story; but presumably the camera
would have recorded something. So the next question that
we must glance at is this: if we are claiming that the Bible
gives us a true account of events by exploring their significance, how far are we committed to believing that anything
actually happened historically? Let us take the example of
the Flood.

If you read the biblical story as a scientific account then
you will have problems, and with these some fundamentalists
have struggled manfully. How many animals could Noah
have got on board? Would the kangaroos have had time to
get there if they had started from Australia the moment that
they were created? One scientist calculated that if the whole
surface of the earth was covered with water, then the orbit of
the earth would have been affected. Now these valiant

attempts to make scientific sense of the story of the Flood look as if they are taking the biblical text seriously, but in fact they are examples of cultural imperialism, the delusion that our way of describing events is the only valid one. We do not have to believe that there was any flood. The biblical author is not claiming that there was one, for the simple reason that it was universally believed in that culture that there had been one. The catastrophe of a universal deluge was simply a common assumption of the time, like that the earth was flat and the heavens a bowl in the sky. The Sumerians and Assyrians and Babylonians all told versions of the Flood story. Even now a team of American archaeologists are searching for the remains of the ark in Turkey. It is unimportant for us whether they find it or not. Given that everyone believed that this catastrophe had taken place, what was at issue was what that said about the relationship between God and human beings. For Israel's neighbours it was evidence that the gods were cruel and arbitrary. They had brought about this flood to rid the earth of these noisy human beings who were spoiling the peace and quiet of the gods. We were only saved from complete destruction by a chance quarrel between the gods. The challenge to the Bible was to show that this story did not necessarily lead to that conclusion. They could hardly pretend that the Flood was positive evidence for God's goodness and kindness, but could suggest that it belonged within a larger story, that stretched from the Fall to the call of Abraham. They reinterpreted it by giving it a different narratival context. So we can see that in this instance the meaning of the story does not demand that anything actually happened historically. A passing cameraman might have been able to record nothing but a bursting of the banks of the Euphrates. It does not follow from a belief in God's love and mercy that there must have been a flood, but if someone happens to believe that there had been a flood, as the Israelites did, then they have to find a place for it within a story that is ultimately one of love and mercy. Of course this interpretation does have remote historical consequences. It would not be true if God did turn out in the end to be cruel and arbitrary. We believe that the story of Jesus shows that he is not, and so, paradoxically, the truth of the story of the Flood is established not by discovering the ark on Mount Ararat but by the resurrection.

In passing we may note that the story of the Flood suggests another sort of difficulty that we may have in reading the Old Testament. Not only is it filled with implausible and mythical events, but we even find God behaving in an apparently cruel and merciless way, wiping out Israel's enemies and slaughtering innocent people on her behalf. The Old Testament is sometimes not just scientifically but morally incredible. We have to remember that Israel always started with the religious assumptions of her neighbours and transformed them. It was simply a given of that culture that the gods were constantly squabbling with each other, and that our battles reflected these celestial tiffs. Israel too believed that her God fought battles but she transformed their significance. God was not just a quarrelsome tyrant forever picking fights. If he wiped out Israel's enemies it was for a purpose, for the sake of his people. Unlike her neighbours Israel believed that God's actions led somewhere, and the canon as a whole discloses that his purposes are all-embracing.

We have been brought back constantly to the resurrection as God's decisive act, and so we must ask ourselves in what sense was that a historical event. If you compare the four gospels it is evident that they cannot all be historically accurate. Mark tells us that the disciples must go to Galilee. There they will see Jesus. Luke tells them not to leave Jerusalem until after Pentecost. Mark tells us, in the original version, that the women were so frightened that they did not say a word to anyone, whereas Matthew has them faithfully deliver the message. John, as always, tells a completely different story from everyone else. No matter how hard one tries it is impossible to fit the four accounts into a single and coherent historical narrative. And since Matthew almost certainly had a copy of the Book of Mark in front of him when he wrote, and Luke, probably, had read both Mark and Matthew, then it seems that they were not too worried about being inconsistent. They have no interest in telling us exactly what happened to the body of Jesus on Easter morning. In fact they go out of their way not to do so. Matthew describes the angel coming down and rolling away the stone from the tomb, but he deliberately does not describe Jesus coming out, unlike the apocryphal Gospel of Peter. In every case the evangelists tell us what really happened by relating the resurrection to the larger story of our redemption, and especially the birth of the Christian community. Matthew typically describes it in terms of the disciples receiving authority to teach; Luke describes the appearance of Jesus to the disciples on the road to Emmaus in terms of the community's celebration of the Eucharist; John describes it as a re-creation of humanity; Jesus breathes his Spirit on the disciples just as God had first made Adam. They never attempt to describe the resurrection as an isolatable event that took place at a particular moment on Easter morning, which might have been witnessed by a casual passer-by. That sort of an account would not tell you what really happened. You can only tell that by placing it within the larger story of our redemption.

This must appear to be an evasion. When we looked at the Flood story we concluded that the only historical consequences were that the resurrection must have taken place; but when we look at the resurrection we are sent back to the larger narrative of the Bible as a whole. Surely with this climactic event, the raising of Jesus, we must be able to point to something having happened. Otherwise in what sense would there have been an event that could have this meaning? I do not think that we can describe the resurrection as a historical event. It is not an event which is simply within our history; it is the beginning of a new history, the new creation. But it does have, surely, historical consequences. If the body of Jesus were still to be lying in the tomb, or if the disciples came in the night and stole it and hid it elsewhere, then it would not have been the sort of event that we claim it to be, God's intervention in our history. That there was an event at all demands, I believe, an empty tomb. Otherwise the disciples were either con-men, or mistaken. But we can only state what sort of an event it was by exploring its meaning in terms of the whole story of redemption, from the creation to the second coming. The evangelists talk about the resurrection

91

by exploring its consequences, the forgiveness of sins and the birth of the Church, but that does not mean that we can reduce it to those consequences, the disciples' feeling that they were forgiven and that the cause of Jesus goes on. A pale analogy would be trying to describe falling in love. I could only describe what happened when I fell in love by talking about how I came to rewrite my whole autobiography. Suddenly I realised where my whole life had been leading, and so on. I would explore the meaning of the event by placing it in the larger story of my whole life. But for it to have been that sort of an event, then certain minimal historical conditions must be met. I must, for example, have met the person in question. Saying that I have met them is no more a description of falling in love with them than saying that the tomb is empty is a description of the resurrection; but they are both necessary conditions for anything significant to have happened in the first place.

To conclude: to believe that the Bible is true is to have confidence that we are saved by Christ's life, death and resurrection. To believe that *everything* in the Bible is true is to believe that it is the whole canon of Scripture that helps us to understand the meaning of that event. Sometimes we may find ourselves plagued by a further and typically modern question: but what really happened? What might I have seen if I had been there? It is a secondary question, one that I rarely find of interest or importance myself, and it is usually unanswerable. But if we find ourselves nagged by it, then all we can do is to ask what *must* have happened if it were to be the sort of event that could have that meaning. We cannot say what did happen when Jesus was raised from the dead, but at least we can say what did not happen. The disciples did not come and hide the body. Or if they did, then it was a con trick, and it could not have been God's intervention in human history to save us.

A test case would be the conception of Jesus. Both Matthew and Luke tell us that Mary conceived Jesus through the power of the Holy Spirit. Clearly they are not interested in the conception as an isolated physiological fact. The story is told because of what it says about Jesus, the one who is of God, the Son of the Father. It articulates their sense of his life as the beginning of something new, a break in a human history of sin and failure. What is at issue is this: could Jesus have had this same significance if, in historical fact, Joseph was his father? Some people will argue that who Jesus is and the meaning of his life, death and resurrection cannot depend upon this purely biological fact. They are asserting that we can be loyal to the truth of the gospels, their sense of Jesus's identity, without being forced to make any bizarre claims about his parentage. I would tend to disagree. The gospels' understanding of Jesus as the only-begotten Son of the Father, the radical novelty of his existence, does seem to imply that we cannot detach the meaning of the story from the historical facts of his origins. Of course the point of the story is not to report a biological fact about his conception but to tell us who Jesus is; but it seems to follow from this sense of who he is that it is right, fitting, *conveniens* (as they would have said in the Middle Ages), to affirm with the tradition that he was truly conceived of the Holy Spirit.

All this must make it sound as if reading the Bible is a very complicated matter for which years of training are required. But it is important to see that the complexity derives not from the Bible but from us. The Bible largely consists of stories. It expounds our faith by telling the story of God's dealing with mankind, and for most people in the world and for most of human history that is a perfectly obvious and proper way to think. If we find it difficult to discover what it means to believe that the Bible is true, it is because in our culture people are frequently driven to ask an odd and eccentric question which it would not occur to most people to raise: but what *really* happened? What would the disinterested spectator have seen? What would the camera have recorded? And if we find it difficult, and sometimes impossible, to answer that question it is not because the Bible is a mysterious and arcane document which only scholars can make sense of. Rather we should ask why we want to ask such a bizarre and complex question.

10

What does it mean to believe in heaven and hell?

To believe in heaven and hell is evidently to make a claim about what will happen to us when we die. As such it is often viewed, even by some Christians, with considerable suspicion. If this world is only a preparation for the next, then is not my present life trivialised? A belief in the afterlife might enter my calculations now, in that I might push myself to do the occasional good deed and restrain myself from committing undetectable crimes so as to gain rewards and escape punishment in the next world, but would it not be nobler to do the right thing just for its own sake? There is something especially inspiring about the atheist who lays down his life for a just cause, believing that he will never see or share in the victory. Against this I would like to argue that belief in heaven and hell gives a heightened sense to what it means for me now to live a human life, take moral decisions and so on. It means that my actions have an intrinsic significance; they matter in themselves and not solely because of what they may lead to.

One of the ways in which we describe what a thing is, what is its nature, is by saying what it needs to be happy, complete. We recognise what a rabbit is when we see that it needs grass, a hole in the ground, some other rabbits and no foxes. That is the sort of environment in which it can flourish and realise its nature. When we say that God has made us to live with him in the kingdom, then we are not just making a statement about what will happen when we die. We are claiming that our present human nature is one that is defined by this destiny. To have a human nature is to be someone who

94

hungers for the life of God and for the perfect peace and justice of the kingdom. Our present human nature is curious and unlike that of the rabbit in that it is defined by the need for that which transcends our nature and which we can only receive as a gift, the sharing in the life of the Trinity. Of course we can hide from an awareness of the deep mystery of our humanity. We can settle for an image of completion found in a life shut off from the rest of mankind and God. We can fool ourselves as to what we want. D. H. Lawrence wrote in his defence of *Lady Chatterley's Lover*:

> All that matters is that men and women should do what they really want to do. Though here as elsewhere [he is talking about sex] we must remember that man has a double set of desires, the shallow and the profound, the personal, superficial, temporary desires, and the inner, impersonal, great desires that are fulfilled in long periods of time. The desires of the moment are easy to recognise, but the others, the deeper ones, are difficult. It is the business of our Chief Thinkers to tell us of our deep desires, not to keep shrilling our little desires in our ears.[1]

In Christianity these deeper desires are identified as a longing for the kingdom of God in which all will be one in Christ. The paradox of our human nature is that it is defined by a longing for what transcends it. Unlike the rabbit we must die to ourselves to be ourselves. So to say that our destiny is heaven is, in the first place, to say something about what it means to be human now. If I find myself discontented with this society, impelled to protest against its injustices, angry with its divisions, then maybe it is not because I am 'maladjusted' or envious, but because of some sense of being made for heaven.

What can we say to those who dismiss this claim that we are destined for heaven as mere escapism, wish fulfilment? Faced with the unhappiness, injustice and misery of this world, we console ourselves with the dream of a better world to come. Since the earthly city turns out to be pretty miserable for some, then we take refuge in the dream of a heavenly city, a new Jerusalem. Freud wrote a book called *The Future of an Illusion*, in which he accepted that religious aspirations were 'the fulfilments of the oldest, strongest, and most urgent wishes of mankind',[2] but to believe that these desires find fulfilment is to succumb to neurotic illusion.

The first and most obvious step to take is to reply that the fact that we want something does not prove that it does not exist. Something that fulfils my deepest desires is not necessarily a projection of my fantasies. I may long for term to be over and the vacation to come, but that does not mean that the holidays are merely a product of my diseased imagination. The fact that heaven would fulfil my deepest longings says, logically, nothing for or against its existence. And surely one could take a further step. If Freud and Marx and Feuerbach are right and this belief in heaven is the surrender to fantasy, then we must admit that most human beings have been profoundly mistaken about their own humanity. Of course it is quite possible for most human beings to be mistaken about something without our fundamental confidence in humanity being undermined. We belong to what is probably that tiny percentage of human beings who believe that the earth is round, but that need not shake our confidence in humanity. But to say that throughout human history we have been wrong to claim that it is with God – or the gods – that we will find happiness is to say that hitherto humanity has been deeply deceived as to what it is to be human. One of the things that would mark us off from rabbits would be that we have been almost universally mistaken as to who and what we are. Of course as Christians we may disagree with others as to what heaven is like; we may feel that the prospect of an eternity of drinking sherbet, as promised by the Koran, or even of hurling golden crowns before the throne of the Lamb, as in the Book of Revelation, hardly measures up to our hopes, but it is another thing to say that human history has been faulted from its earliest beginnings by an illusory yearning. It would be paradoxical to invite us to leave behind the illusion of heaven and live in the truth while, at the same time, effectively making a vote of no confidence in our ability to do so.

96

Even harder to understand is the position of those Christians who maintain that it is an illusion to believe in an afterlife. If God is our creator, then it is hard to see why he would have created us with deep aspirations that are bound to be frustrated. If we have this yearning for transcendence, and believe in the creator God, then it makes sense to believe that we will attain what we long for. So once one has made the step of believing in God at all then the fact that heaven would be a wish-fulfilment is positively an argument in favour of its existence.

At the heart of this dismissal of belief in heaven is usually the suspicion that it has harmful consequences; it is likely to distract us from the real task of the Christian, which is the transformation of this world. Even if heaven were to exist it would be undesirable to focus our attention on it. The poor endure an injustice and a poverty that they ought to challenge because they comfort themselves with the dream of the next life, so in actual practice belief in heaven works in favour of the rich by acting as a palliative for the sufferings of the poor. If one factor to be taken into account in an assessment of validity of a doctrine is its social consequences, then surely belief in heaven has a lot working against it. It can discourage us from taking responsibility for our world, and even encourage people to act disastrously. Many people probably fail to register the enormity of the crime of using a nuclear bomb against our enemies because they believe that God will raise everyone from the dead anyway. One could argue that a belief in heaven may cheapen our sense of the value of human life. And so it is suggested that now that we have come of age, and as a sign of our maturity, we can dispense with the afterlife. Don Cupitt, for example, said: 'It is spiritually important that one should *not* believe in life after death but instead strive to attain the goal of life in history.'[3] We can sympathise with Cupitt's concern over the effect of a belief in heaven. Of course the fact that we may feel reservations at the effect of belief in it does not actually prove that it does not exist, and anyway I believe that, properly understood, an awareness of heaven as the destiny that God intends for mankind has quite the opposite consequences to those

suggested by Cupitt and others. It grants a value and serious-
ness to the moral decisions that we take. It safeguards us
from trivialising this world as a sphere of moral actions.

It might help us to see why this is so if we glance, very
briefly, at how Israel came to believe in the resurrection in
the first place. For most of her history Israel believed that
after death all that awaited one was Sheol. Sheol was like the
Greek Hades, a shadowy place, where everyone, good and
bad, rich and poor, ended up living a sort of half-existence.
The most that an Israelite could hope for was that his or her
name would be remembered by the clan or the tribe, a future
given in the continuity of the people. They lived on in their
name. The story of how Israel came to develop a firm belief
in resurrection is long and complex but, at the risk of over-
simplification, there were three principal factors, each of
which suggests that this went with a heightened sense of the
importance of our individual moral decisions in this world:
political oppression, a growing sense of the significance of the
individual and a developed theology of God as the creator.
Each factor was indispensable. One of the earliest clear refer-
ences to the resurrection is in the Book of Daniel, which
reflects the crisis of the nation when the temple was desecrated
by Antiochus Epiphanes, the Syrian king. Loyal Jews were
being forced to renounce the law and conform to Hellenistic
mores. It was no longer enough just to be born a Jew, they
had to consciously choose a Jewish identity. Obedience to the
law was a matter of an individual choice which frequently
entailed death. But inevitably the question was asked: What
was the point in dying rather than eating pork? What good
did it do? It clearly did not contribute to a national revival.
One of the factors that seems to have given an impetus to
belief in the resurrection was the sense that the individual
heroic decision to cleave to the law, however useless and
fruitless it seemed to be, was of inherent value. It was enough
to do the right thing, regardless of the consequences. And
this perception of the value of the individual deed could only
have been articulated as a belief in the resurrection if Israel
had acquired a deep sense that God was the source and the
origin of all that exists. God could only be believed in as re-

creator if he had first been accepted as creator. Look at this speech from the Second Book of Maccabees, of a mother who has watched her seven children die because they would not eat pork:

> I do not know how you came into being in my womb. It was not I who gave you life and breath, nor I who set in order the elements within each of you. Therefore the creator of the world, who shaped the beginning of man and devised the origin of all things, will in his mercy give life and breath back to you again, since you now forget yourselves for the sake of his laws. (7:22–3)

So the growth of belief in the resurrection did not derive from a flight from the significance of this world. On the contrary it depended upon a heightened sense that we as individuals, and our moral struggles, matter, and that we can trust in God since he is the creator and the origin of all that is.

With Christianity this sense of the intrinsic value of our actions is deepened, and this is partly because the resurrection is no longer seen as a purely future event, an 'afterlife' that makes sense of the pointless absurdity of the martyrs' deaths; the resurrection, eternal life, is something that we enter now, by being baptised into Christ's dying and rising. Our actions acquire a new weight, since they belong to dying with Christ and the present inbreaking of the kingdom. As it says in the First Letter of John: 'We know that we have passed out of death into life, because we love the brethren' (3:14). Dying and rising are part of the present drama of our lives. The idea that it is part of the vocation of the Christian to die with Christ is deeply embedded in the New Testament and our tradition. We can find it in Paul, for example: 'If we have died with Christ, we believe that we shall also live with him' (Rom. 6:8), and it is still there in John's Gospel (12:24) where Jesus invites us to be like the seed that must fall into the ground and die if it is not to be alone. With Christianity death becomes, like eternal life, not just the end of our existence but a way of being. But we have to be extremely careful how we understand this way of talking. It is so easily mistaken for something completely different, and to which it is radically opposed, a self-hatred, a longing for extinction. This is a confusion that we are especially likely to make these days since one of the characteristic temptations of this age is to hold oneself to be worthless. Deep self-doubt is an awful burden for so many people, and often the gospel has to challenge us to overcome that and to love ourselves as our neighbour. Dying to ourselves with Christ is nothing to do with cultivating a death wish. The gospels invite us to seek life and not extinction. So often people have endured inhuman situations in which they have been unable to flourish, wives have submitted to tyranny, for example, because that looked like obedience to the gospel invitation to die with Christ, self-denial. But dying with Christ is not masochism or self-repression; it is more the slow and painful process of being born, coming to life. It is not the negation of this life for the sake of the next, but the present breaking in of God into our lives. 'If a man loves me, he will keep my word, and my Father will love him and we will come to him and make our home with him' (John 14:23). Loving acts acquire an intrinsic value, regardless of what they ultimately achieve, as being sacramental of God's dwelling with mankind now. To confess a belief in heaven is, for a Christian, to claim the proper value and significance of our deeds as the making flesh, the incarnation, of eternal life.

If we reject a belief in heaven and argue that we must instead concentrate on building a heaven on earth, then the value of our actions must remain uncertain. A good action may turn out to have been pointless in the light of history. A belief in heaven means that our actions have a value even if our goals are frustrated. Not because God will have noted them down and will reward us, but because any act of love is of its nature part of the coming of the kingdom, God's dwelling with mankind. Let us imagine that you help someone to get off the streets, give up drink and rebuild their lives. It is always possible, and will often happen in my experience, that one day they will turn up at the door again, drunk and apparently back where they started. Do you then decide that it was a waste of time to have helped them? Is that act of love emptied of significance? To believe with the New Testament in the present inbreaking of God is to claim that it has a value quite simply as an act of love, a sacrament of the kingdom.

We are more likely to see this dying with Christ as a self-hatred, a longing for oblivion, if we see our human nature as something intrinsically wicked from which God needs to rescue us. But this would be to misunderstand what it means to be human. We started by suggesting that we have a nature only in a rather curious sense of the word. It belongs to our humanity to reach out beyond ourselves for what we can only receive as a gift. The contented rabbit is simply itself, but we have, in the depths of our humanity, the hunger for something more, the life of the Trinity. Lawrence said, you may remember, 'All that matters is that men and women should do what they really want to do.' The new Testament invitation to die with Christ offers a way to realise our deepest desire for life, for the fullness of life. Baptism is not a moment in which we shed a wicked humanity; it is the midwife in our coming to be, the grace that perfects our nature. Since I have quoted one Cambridge don (Don Cupitt) for the opposition, let me show how broad-minded I am by quoting another with approval, Nicholas Lash:

> There seems to be a sense in which, without the willingness to die, human existence remains mere 'existence' and cannot flourish, cannot 'come alive'. In our relationships with other people, with new ideas and the challenge of fresh situations, we have continuously to risk the unknown, the unfamiliar, the disturbing. We have to risk the destruction of whatever 'safe little world' we have so far succeeded in carving out of chaos. The person who has not the courage thus to risk 'dying' throughout his life is unlikely to have the courage to die at the end. The person who has not the courage to live for other people, the courage to risk the unknown, the courage to risk relationship – and thereby to risk the 'death' of separation or betrayal – will not have the courage to die into the arms of God. The person who

tries to live 'privately', to hang on to his possessions, his friendships, his certainties, will die privately, alone, and this is hell.[4]

This, then, brings me to hell. I believe that we must believe in hell for the same reason that we believe in heaven, since it is the ground of our understanding of the proper value and significance of human actions. In a novel called *Love Among the Ruins*, Evelyn Waugh describes the sad case of an ancient criminal who, after a life dedicated to crime, finds himself sent out to a reformatory, where kind people try to cure him of his illness. But Mr Sweat does not appreciate this dedication to his well-being:

'I'll tell you what it is, chum,' continued Mr Sweat, 'There's no understanding of crime these days like there was. I remember when I was a nipper, the first time I came up before the beak, he spoke up straight: "My lad," he says, "you are embarking upon a course of life that can only lead to disaster and degradation in this world and everlasting damnation in the next." Now that's talking. It's plain sense and it shows a personal interest. But the last time I was up, when they sent me here, they called me an "antisocial phenomenon", said I was "maladjusted". That's no way to speak of a man what was doing time before they was in long trousers, now is it?'[5]

Of course Mr Sweat is unaware that one of the most important insights of the last century is into how far we are in fact formed and moulded by our upbringing, the language and perception that we inherit, and by factors beyond our control. That is the context within which we are free. The doctrine of hell only makes sense to me as an assertion of our dignity as those who are, in the end, free to choose.

The traditional imagery of hell is almost certain to obscure the proper meaning of the doctrine. The idea that people might be subjected to eternal punishment is repellent, even though Tertullian believed that it would be one of the joys of heaven for us to contemplate the sufferings of the damned.

Hell seems to be incompatible with a belief in a God of mercy. The mistake would be, I suspect, to think that this doctrine is primarily saying something about the nature of God, such as that there is a limit to his mercy. It is the clear teaching of the New Testament that there is no end or limit to God's mercy. This doctrine of hell is in the first place saying something about us, that we are free to decide whether to enter the kingdom or not. It celebrates our dignity. Of course that does in turn imply something important about what it means to say that God loves us; it does not imply that there is a limit to God's love, but that it is not a paternalistic love that would sweep us into his presence against our will. It is the love of a father who would bring us into freedom. The doctrine of hell is a protest against paternalism.

It may help to bear in mind the origins of this traditional imagery of unending fire and eternal worms. They probably derive from the last verses of Isaiah, in which he describes corpses lying unburied in the Hinnon valley near Jerusalem: 'And they shall go forth and look on the dead bodies of the men who have rebelled against me; for their worm shall not die, their fire shall not be quenched, and they shall be an abhorrence to all flesh' (66:24). The point about the fire and the worms is not that they are a punishment; they are a sign that these bodies are not yet buried. They have just been dumped on a smouldering, maggot-ridden rubbish tip. For a Jew, as for all the people of the ancient Near East, burial was the completion of the process of dying. They could not find rest until they were laid in the earth; neither properly dead nor alive. What is abhorrent about these bodies is that they are just decomposing, unburied; they have not attained the peace of death. And that is a good image of hell, the failure to die; or, if that seems too close in our minds to the temptation of a death-wish, the failure to be born. Herbert McCabe, OP says in his new catechism; 'If we die rejecting God's gift of the Spirit we are unable to accept death, so that it remains our enemy for ever. This is called hell.'[6] Once again, this dying has nothing to do with self-hatred or the yearning for oblivion; it belongs to our being reborn into each other's company, the end of solitude. 'Unless a grain of wheat falls into the ground and dies, it remains alone' (John 12:24). We do not have to believe that anyone will go to hell; it may be that no one ever has or will use their freedom in this way. But we need to believe in both heaven and hell to retain a proper sense of the significance and value of our human lives.

Notes

1. D. H. Lawrence, *Apropos of Lady Chatterley's Lover*. 1931. Quoted by H. McCabe, *Law, Love and Language*. 1968.

2. S. Freud, 'The Future of an Illusion', *Standard Edition of the Complete Psychological Works of Sigmund Freud*. 1953.

3. Don Cupitt, *Taking Leave of God*. 1980.

4. Nicholas Lash, *Theology on Dover Beach*. 1979.

5. Evelyn Waugh, *Love Among the Ruins*. 1962.

6. Herbert McCabe, OP, *The Teaching of the Catholic Church: a New Catechism of Christian Doctrine*. 1985.

11

Exploration in community: why the Church?

'You will need a bit of passion along with Runcie coolness', the Archbishop of Canterbury had written to me when we were discussing Encounters two years previously; and it was he who suggested teaming him with MYRA BLYTH the Baptist minister who is Youth Secretary of the British Council of Churches. Here they both examine the nature of the community whose task it is to point to the love of God and make it recognisable to the world. Each, Anglican and Baptist, chooses to speak of the Church as the eucharistic community.

I. The Archbishop

I began in Chapter 1 by talking about belief, about why and what I believe, and with the help of others we have been exploring further such fundamental questions about the Christian faith. Now, last of all, 'Why the Church?'

The broadcaster Gerald Priestland has posed the question, 'Who needs the Church?':

Do you? Do I? Does God? Does anybody need the Church except the Church itself? Has it ever been anything but a gigantic confidence trick, a home for old ladies, a career structure for sentimental wets, surviving on a mixture of superstition, toadyism, and spiritual blackmail? . . . Not to mention the crusades and persecutions, the wars of religion, the inquisitions and heresy hunts, the martyrdoms and book-burnings. Who needs a Church like this? Was this what Jesus of Nazareth had in mind – Jesus who walked the hills of Palestine, teaching in the open air, sharing his bread and wine with his friends, and passing on his gospel to twelve ordinary working men?[1]

The popularity of Priestland's programmes has caused Dr Edward Norman to declare that the British people have deposed the Archbishop of Canterbury and elected Priestland as the nation's spiritual leader – so that's my excuse for quoting him here, and at length.

And, what's more, I have much sympathy with his doubts and questions. There's much to shame and embarrass us in the Church and its history. There's a Latin tag, *corruptio optimi pessima* – roughly translated, 'when the best goes bad, all hell is let loose'.

But these are the scars and scandals – serious and tragic enough, but they do not destroy the Church. Even out of the most evil times saints have been born to restore the vision – a mystery which defies explanation and has fascinated the artist and author from Dostoevsky to Graham Greene.

So what is the vision? I am talking as much about how the Church is *meant* to be, and *can* be, and sometimes *is*. In trying to answer the question, 'Why the Church?' I'm going to explore how it is that this community has such an essential, crucial, indispensable part to play in all that God is accomplishing in the world through Jesus Christ, through his life and death and resurrection.

Let me begin with Jesus sharing his bread and wine with his friends. That simple commonplace action of Jesus on the night he was betrayed gave birth to the central, characteristic act of Christian worship. The mass, the Eucharist, the Lord's supper, the liturgy, Holy Communion – call it what you will. For me this is the heart of the matter – this same simple action of Jesus, but repeated, elaborated and filled with inexhaustible significance in every age and in every place on earth.

One of the unusual and exciting experiences of an archbishop is that he shares in this service often enough, but very seldom in the same place or in exactly the same way. As I look back a year or so I remember taking part in it informally in a hotel bedroom in China, where the Church, after the cultural revolution, is like a patient recovering from a near-fatal illness. So, as we met together, it seemed ridiculous that I should say to any of those around the table: 'by the way, are you a Methodist?' or, 'incidentally, are you a Catholic?' or, 'you look like an Anglican'. Then I have taken part in it with thousands in a stadium in Nigeria where the amazing growth of the Church gives an exuberance and liveliness that overwhelm the visitor. On that occasion they floated balloons around the stadium to welcome me. They were stamped with my image and sold with the ambiguous caption: 'Help the Anglican Communion and blow up the Archbishop of Canterbury'! Or in Bulgaria where, as in the Soviet Union, there was something haunting and timeless about the chanting and the flickering candles, in sharp contrast to a world outside of new hydro-electric plants and muscular statues of State heroes which seemed to proclaim with Swinburne: 'This thing is God. To be man with all thy might'. And of course at home I have shared it with stately English restraint in Canterbury Cathedral. Or when, instead of going to my chapel, I slip into my local inner-city Lambeth church where the devotion of a tiny and remarkable little group in their vast echoing building seems strangely more powerful than the packed houses which sometimes greet me.

It is through sharing above all in the Eucharist that the Christian community is reminded again and again of the story of Jesus, of his life and especially his death. This is crucial – for what a person remembers, regularly and easily, makes him into the kind of person he is. The bread, taken and broken, brings to mind that body broken on the cross at Calvary. The wine, blessed and shared, brings to mind the blood shed on Good Friday – for us men and for our salvation. The Eucharist, the communion, is a *sacrament*, an outward and visible sign or symbol by which we remember with thanks the infinite love of God which moved him to suffering and sacrifice. As we eat and drink the bread and wine, so we are to enter into this love and this love into us – nourishing and strengthening our faith and transforming our lives, empowering the Church to live with something of the same

107

courage and generosity, the same faith, love and gentleness of Christ.

'For as often', says St Paul, 'as you eat this bread and drink this cup, you proclaim the Lord's death until he comes.' The Eucharist is a sign to Christ *within* the Church and *for* the Church – it keeps the Church constantly in touch with its Founder and Lord, and true to his message and the pattern of his life and death.

But the Eucharist is a sacrament within a sacrament. For the Church – and this is my second point – is itself a sacrament. It is the sign of the grace and goodness of God: the Church exists in the world to re-present to each generation the saving life and love of Jesus, crucified and risen. To put the matter more simply, the Church is to be that 'thing' in the world by which the love of God can be recognised for what it is. The Church is that 'place' in the world where God's love can become identifiable. The Church, said Archbishop William Temple, is the only society which exists for those who are not (yet) its members.

Take first the Church at worship and prayer. The Christian community meeting together on the Lord's day around the Lord's table to share the Lord's supper; the Church's art and architecture and music which enrich and inspire its worship, and speak so eloquently of the beauty and holiness of God – all these things can be signs to the world of God's existence, of his disclosure in Christ, and of the response of wonder and love he evokes in his creation.

And then the Church is called to be *active* in the world, active in service, proclaiming by what it does and by the stand it takes something of the same love and courage and sacrifice of Christ.

A Christian [wrote Dietrich Bonhoeffer] must live a worldly life and so participate in the suffering of God. To be a Christian does not mean to be religious in a particular way . . . but to be a man. It is not some religious act which makes a Christian what he is, but participation in the suffering of God in the life of the world.[2]

This, of course, will involve the Church in politics. That is unavoidable, though it is not always welcomed or appreciated. I remember how one year a certain Member of Parliament called upon the Church to give up politics for Lent!

Let me give you an example of the Church's task. Let us take circumstances which are difficult for the Church – say a decaying area of the inner city, where the Church seems weak, and where all around is deprivation, poverty, conflict – all that the Bible means by 'injustice'. I take it as beyond question that the God of the Bible is on the side of justice and that his Church, wherever it is, must be on the side of justice. A Church which averts its eyes and draws in its skirts from injustice on its doorstep is not the Church of the God the prophets proclaimed and Jesus disclosed. Both corporately and individually the Church is bound to do whatever it can, in private and in public, to uphold and advance the cause of justice against injustice. Justice is the coin in which the currency of love is paid out in a world of complex systems.

Of course, the Church is never the *only* agency of justice, and it would be gravely deluding itself if it thought it was. In every place great good is done by organisations and individuals quite unconnected with the Church. The will of God is often carried out by people who do not mention his name or even recognise his existence. Because such people exist, and because in numbers and resources they often far outweigh the Church, the Church cannot possibly make a realistic claim to be the *one and only* agency through which God imparts his love and goodness to the world.

But what the Church *can* claim to be is what it is intended to be: the sacrament of the love and grace of God. The calling of the Church is to be the 'thing', the place, the activity, the community, through which the love of God in Christ becomes *recognisable* for what it is. Certainly God's love reaches the world in many forms and through many agencies: but often it comes unrecognised. Through the Church, through its saints and martyrs, past and present, as well as through the lives of ordinary Christian men and women, that love and compassion can be recognised, received and celebrated.

At the end of his review of Christianity and History, the

Cambridge historian Herbert Butterfield has a passage like this:

> It's not so important that any *one* form of Christianity should succeed in the world – or that they should make mistakes in mundane matters – as that there should be Christians in the world, proclaiming the gospel, nourishing the pieties, practising New Testament love, affirming the spiritual nature of man.
>
> This is the spring which is ever generative of new things – at one time education, in another Red Cross work, or scientific method, a form of art, or social justice. In time they will sail off under other auspices, but Christians are to guard the spring – I would say to be the sign of a divine presence among all the agonies and perplexities of our world.[3]

There is a marvellous prayer towards the end of the modern Anglican Communion Service. I want to finish by quoting it because it summarises so well all I have been trying to say:

> Father of all, we give you thanks and praise, that when we were still far off you met us in your son and brought us home. Dying and living, he declared your love, gave us grace, and opened the gate of glory. May we who share Christ's body live his risen life; we who drink his cup bring life to others; we whom the Spirit lights give light to the world. Keep us firm in the hope you have set before us, so we and all your children shall be free, and the whole earth live to praise your name through Christ our Lord. Amen.[4]

II. The Revd Myra Blyth

The Church is a dynamic community. It may have escaped your notice, but it is. The Church in the New Testament at least promises us that, and indeed the words that are used are very strongly dynamic. Instead of 'Church' we should really read 'assembly' or 'congregation', meaning 'the coming together of people'; and as far as I am concerned (from what I understand from Scripture) the Church exists when people come together.

The Church is not bricks and mortar, but flesh and blood. The Church lives and breathes and has its being when people come together and have God at the centre. Many people when they bother to ask the question, 'Why the Church?' end up walking away and shrugging their shoulders and saying, 'Why bother?' For when they look at the Church they cannot see that dynamism, they cannot see anything except people coming together for some very strange reasons, but it does not really look particularly dynamic, and therefore not much to do with their lives.

A recent survey by the British Council of Churches amongst teenagers in the Church reveals just what they think of the Church. It shows that 71 per cent of young people who go to church at the age of thirteen will have left by the age of nineteen: 71 per cent. The Church of England does worst in the attendance stakes because they lose 75 per cent and the Catholics about 63 per cent and the Free Churches 59 per cent; so none of them have much to crow about. What seems significant is that young people are voting with their feet. If they do not feel that they belong, and clearly they do not, if they have not discovered the dynamic quality of a Church that exists as a body, in which there is equal status of all the members, then they will vote with their feet; and they have done so.

When it comes to the question of belief amongst these young people who still are hanging on with the Church, there were also some interesting statistics. It seems that most of the young people who go to church are perfectly happy to assent to most of the creeds. Only 3 per cent of those surveyed did not believe in God, 2 per cent rejected belief in Jesus as the Son of God – I should underline that this was young people who were being surveyed – and 4 per cent rejected outright a belief in the physical resurrection of Jesus. Now those were fairly low statistics. The majority of young people were assenting to the basic tenets of the faith. We may consider that to be good news, but I wonder what it says when we

111

recall William Temple's comment that the Church exists for the benefit of those who are not in it. I would very much like to see higher statistics, if higher statistics were actually to say we were taking seriously, and able to embrace within the Church, young people who do not accept the faith, and are in themselves seeking for a true faith. If all we have are people who think in the same way, then perhaps we are not taking seriously our pastoral and our evangelistic task. But more significant still was the revelation from this particular survey that 50 per cent of the young people in the Church may assent to the tenets of the faith but they do not think they have ever had a spiritual experience. What does that say about the Church? Whatever else we are doing, it does not appear to be the case that we are enabling people to make sense of their spiritual lives.

I think Kenneth Leech in his book, *The Social God*, puts his finger on one of the reasons for this. He says there is a sense in which the clergy and perhaps the leaders within the Church have backed away from the primary task of the Church, which is to offer spiritual guidance and spiritual awareness. It does seem to me significant in what is described as a deeply spiritual age, that 50 per cent of those young people in the Church do not feel they have been helped to make sense of it. I opened a youth culture magazine called 'I.D.' and the total middle section of that magazine was on spiritual awareness; anything from Christianity to tree worship was defined. It was not attempting to be a sop to the Christian Church: it was attempting to meet what it reckons is popular thinking amongst young people, and it was looking at spiritual awareness. Yet 50 per cent of our young people are not aware of spiritual experiences.

Worst of all within the report of what these young people perceived and thought of the Church was the fact that when the survey went out 40 per cent of the churches refused to do it, because it asked some sensitive questions about relationships and sex; and the clergy in their wisdom said to the researcher, 'These questions are beyond the experience of our young people.' That says more to me about the adult Church than it does about the youth. What was very clear from those who did answer the questions was that they wanted much more opportunity to talk about social and political issues from a perspective of faith. They wanted the opportunity to talk about relationships and sex and abortion, the occult, the cults, as well as prayer and the Bible. Of those young people, 71 per cent were leaving, I believe, because the Church is still falling very far short of its ideal. The Archbishop of Canterbury confesses the inadequacy of the Church in the past. I believe we have a great deal of confessing to do even now, when we are losing so many young people and engaging in dialogue with fewer still.

But if all that is the depressing side, I would want to share with you that my understanding of the Church, like that of the Archbishop, goes to the central theme and the central story, and it is from this that I believe we have a vision and a programme for the Church which is possible. Perhaps it seems a bit strange for someone coming from a Free Church, even more strange from a Baptist Church, to be saying that I believe the Church is not only a dynamic community, I believe the Church is a *eucharistic* community. But maybe three years in the ecumenical movement has helped me to look again at exactly what we are doing when we eat bread and drink wine; and I want to commend to you what I have learned about the Eucharist. I want to offer it to you and ask you to think what it is in our understanding of this central story which is both the proclamation of the gospel and the living-out of the gospel. What is it that prevents us from sharing it together? Because that, if anything, is the scandal of the Church in its image to the world.

Sharing bread and drinking wine is the central act of the Christian Church. During the first Holy Week Christ said, 'Do this', and ever since we have dutifully done it. But why? What does it mean? When we go back to the original testimonies in the New Testament we discover that the writers of the four gospels and Paul are at pains to describe Jesus's actions rather than his words. The Lord Jesus took bread. He didn't just pass on sayings, he passed on *actions*, and the emphasis right the way through, in my view, is on what he did rather than what he said. If we can be agreed on that,

113

then the squabbles of the Church down the centuries have been about the wrong thing.

Jesus said, 'Do this': again and again we read it. What did he do? Four things. He received; he gave thanks; he broke; and he shared. Actions and picture stories were the ways in which Jesus communicated. Do you remember that road to Emmaus? As Jesus walked along the road with the disciples, they felt they knew him but they did not quite get it together until they went into the house. There Jesus broke bread; and the gospel writer says it was in the breaking of bread that they recognised him, that their eyes were opened. It was the actions that worked. Clearly the old adage, 'Actions speak louder than words', has more than a passing relevance when it comes to the eucharistic meal. The emphasis upon actions for me changes the whole character, the whole significance of the event. It shifts the emphasis away from a memory – which is a very difficult thing in Free Churches – it is more than a remembrance, it is a celebration, it is a dynamic experience.

When Christ says, 'Do this', he is saying much more than simply, 'Eat bread and drink wine'. In the actions which make up that meal Jesus was focusing upon the very gestures that made up his life. Receiving, thanking, breaking and sharing are the qualities which are now enacting out the whole of his life. So when he says to us, 'Do this', he is saying: 'Take on these marks of my discipleship and make them yours.' When Jesus says, 'Do this', and we eat bread and drink wine, we are actually entering into the prelude to the Eucharist. The Orthodox Church talks about the liturgy after the liturgy. Now, I probably do not fully understand what they mean by it, but what I *think* they mean is that the meal is actually about a sacramental lifestyle, and the validity of the Eucharist is realised and actualised when it flows out into our daily living. Whoever eats bread and drinks wine and, dare I say it, whoever consecrates it, is not the fundamental question. It is whether what we have done together is realised and therefore validated in the lives that we live. Inasmuch as we can learn in our lives to receive, then it becomes real. Inasmuch as we are willing to be broken and poured out, the Eucharist is real.

Let us look at those gestures. On the whole we are not very good at *receiving*; the Protestant work ethic has told us for many years now that dignity is earned, and it is far superior to earn than it is to receive. Indeed it seems a sign of deficiency or weakness in us if we need to receive from others. I travelled to Ballymeena and was taken round the town by a Presbyterian minister. He showed me seven of the Presbyterian churches in the town, and then he told me that he had met three of the Presbyterian ministers. When I registered some surprise that he had only actually met three of his own colleagues, he said, 'Oh, it's really quite easy. You see, we're all strong enough anyway, we don't need each other.' Well, that is true enough, the magic figure did seem to be about 800 apiece, but that still did not seem to me to explain it fully. Because there comes a point when we become so comfortable, numerically or materially or even spiritually, that we no longer put ourselves in a position to receive from each other, as individuals in our relationships, or as churches. Receiving is an action which is a sign of the Eucharist being made real in our lives.

Thanking is an equally difficult gesture. Such is our confusion that we spend the first five years of our lives being told, 'What do you say?' 'Thank you'; and from that point on we are told we should never need to have to say thank you again. Our whole education system is about standing on our own two feet: 'Show what you're made of!' Simon the Pharisee found the woman's gratitude to Jesus totally distasteful and humiliating. It seemed to him quite indecent ever to need to have to be so much in someone's debt. Whether it is pride or ignorance within us I do not know, but, while we may have learned on one occasion how to say 'thank you', it seems that we have long since forgotten. When we consider the blatant destruction of total forests, the elimination of a thousand species every year, the rampant pollution of the earth, it demonstrates by our deeds that giving thanks is something we might speak about but we do not live. And it reminds me that when we offer thanks for bread and wine through that traditional Jewish prayer we are actually committing ourselves to a quality of stewardship which calls

115

for radical personal and social change. If we really mean 'thank you', then we live it.

The action of *breaking*, even more than receiving and thanking, speaks of the costliness of Jesus's sacrifice. Bonhoeffer spoke of the cheap grace that the Church so often is happy to offer. In contrast Jesus shows us the way in which to break systems and to be broken, and he knew what it was like; and the real Church, the prophetic Church, the dynamic living Church, is one that is brave enough to stand up against systems and to break systems. Someone said to me that they reckoned we are perhaps moving into what might be another age for the confessing Church, the Church being willing to stand up and make its voice and its actions evident. The task of breaking is not however a purely negative action: it is a positive one. Jeremiah the prophet destroyed a vessel, not to throw it away but to start again, and to make it yet more perfect.

And lastly, *sharing*. Of these four gestures which show the real character of the Church through Christ's own body, sharing is the most natural of the gestures we can hope to perform because, as my Orthodox friends have taught me, God is a community of three, Father, Son and Holy Spirit. God knows himself and relates to himself in community. If we are made in the image of God, then we can only truly reflect the communal nature of God when we live out our lives in relation to each other. Not in isolation, but in communion with each other. Sadly it has become for us a most difficult and self-conscious gesture, because everything about our culture praises individualism and competition rather than compassion and community.

This way of understanding the sacraments, which are the heart of the Church and the nature of the Church; this way of understanding the sacrament of bread and wine, is so very important because for me it gives a real place to a practical response to the gift of God in redemption, Christ's commitment to transforming the world and ours as the Church through him. For me a real picture of community is found in the Bible but elsewhere also. One of my favourite books is Kenneth Grahame's *Wind in the Willows*. Very early on in that novel you will recall that Mole and Rat go out in a boat together into the middle of the river. Mole lives in the ground and Rat lives in the water, so Rat has taken Mole out. And Mole says, 'So this is a river!' '*The* river,' replied Rat, 'I live in it. It's my aunt, my uncle, my cousins. What it doesn't know isn't worth knowing. What it hasn't got isn't worth having. It's eating, it's drinking, it's actually my washing too. It's everything. Lord, the times we've had together!'

That to me is a picture of true community. Rat recognised his total dependence on the world of the river bank, and rejoiced and celebrated in that dependence. Now just as a fish needs water, and a bird needs air, so our natural environment as the people of God, as the Church of God, is to live and breathe and have our being in the body of Christ: to be unashamed and to celebrate that, and to be able to share it without hypocrisy in a world that looks on and wonders why we bother. We bother because Christ has given us a vision which one day will be realised, and then the Church which is now very provisional will be complete and beautiful.

Notes

1. Gerald Priestland, 'Who Needs The Church?' Address in Great St Mary's, Cambridge (10 October 1982).
2. Dietrich Bonhoeffer, *Letters and Papers from Prison*. 1953.
3. Herbert Butterfield, *Christianity and History*. 1949.
4. Holy Communion, Rite A, Alternative Service Book. 1980.